The Laws of Triathlon

By Volker Winkler & Robyn Hatler

Illustrations By Kim Boyd

Dedicated to fellow triathletes, family, friends, volunteers and spectators, who make the sport what it is today.

And for all those cyclists who think their sh*t don't stink.

Endorsements

"What I like best about *The Laws of Triathlon* is how the authors have managed to impute pearls of wisdom while poking fun at those of us who take our sport – and our lives – too seriously. Often the best vehicle to pass on information is self-effacing humor. And this book does it well."
– Scott Tinley, Ph.D.
Two Time Winner of Ironman World Championship

"Volker and Robyn have written an entertaining, but essential guide for triathletes new and old. Their "laws" for triathlon swimming – many addressing issues you might not think of – will help you prepare before race day to have a more successful and enjoyable experience on the day."
– Terry Laughlin,
Founder of Total Immersion

"*The Laws of Triathlon* is a fun and insightful read for triathletes of all abilities, and a light-hearted rebuttal to cycling's "*The Rules*" by Velominati."
– James Loaring,
Triathlon Canada Age Group Coach of the Year

Contents

Acknowledgments

There is no way we could have completed this book on our own. The "Laws" are a result of experiences - some our own, some witnessed and most shared. For most of our "Laws" we tried to give credit where credit was due. A number of spectacular people allowed us to use their quotes and experiences to give some credibility to the "Laws." There were a couple in which it was a challenge to quote them directly, as we had a shared experience with a situation that they have written about.

One is Jesse Thomas. Jesse is a four time champion (as of 2016) of the Wildflower Long Course Triathlon (a world famous triathlon that is on most triatletes' bucket list). Not only is he a pro triathlete and the CEO of Picky Bars, he is also one of the most down-to-earth people you will ever meet. Not that I have met him personally, but you can tell from his correspondence. I feel that if I showed up on Jesse's doorstep he would invite me in for coffee and be willing to spare whatever time he had (not that he would have a lot of spare time) to not just talk about himself but would want to know all about me. If you doubt my sincerity you should check out his articles in "Triathlete Magazine." He is a regular contributor and his articles will have you laughing out loud, taking notes or both. In particular his article in "Triathlete February 2014: What I Wish I'd Known" and his article in "Triathlete August 2014" that highlighted "Terrible Triathlon Advice" gave us fuel to include some "Laws." If you have a pro triathlete giving you the same advice as what you believe other triathletes should know, then it must be a "Law."

Of course, we also need to acknowledge the authors of "The Rules" because without coming across that book we may have never realized that triathletes also had a "code" they abided by. Not to mention after reading "The Rules" we were a little upset that we could not be considered a true cyclist according *to their standards. So, what do you do when you aren't allowed into your neighbor's fort - you make your own.*

We would also like to acknowledge Christopher McDougall, Bob Babbitt, Matt Fitzgerald, Bobby McGee, Shane Eversfield, Karen Smyers, Joe Friel, Chrissie Wellington, Leanda Cave, Chris McCormack and Mark Allen, as we utilized some of their quotes that effectively reinforced our "Laws."

Last but not least we need to acknowledge our family and friends some of whom contributed to the "Laws" knowingly and some who contributed as a result of our witnessing their experiences. - Robyn

The coolest thing about acknowledging these people is that it reinforces the very essence of triathlon - pros, veterans, newbies, serious age groupers and the weekend warriors. We are all united by our love of the crazy sport of triathlon.

A special thank you to our triathlete friends whose names we have used without even thinking of asking their permission. If you don't like what we said – be thankful it could have been a lot worse. Thank you for all the miles of shared experiences. Thank you to those that read our initial manuscript - Kirsten Sass, David and Angela Hacker, Marilyn Horn and Bertha Robles. Your input was much appreciated and implemented. Thank you to Kim Boyd for her original illustrations. Thank you to my kids - Kirsten, Jesse, Benjamin, Ty, Robyn and Roman - who tolerated and supported us through numerous dinner table discussions. Thank you especially to Robyn, without whom this book never would have been written. Just like my triathlons it was a slow but a fun journey. - Volker

Introduction

Things once seen cannot be unseen. When a fellow triathlete's wet suit is stripped beside you and he has forgotten to wear his shorts, the image will be forever burned into your brain. So it was for me, immediately followed by the thought that there should be a "law" against that type of display and that someone is going to have a most memorable bike ride.

Years have passed since that fateful morning and since then I have been exposed to numerous other questionable behaviors by triathletes. A book of "laws" has yet to surface. In 2013, *"The Rules: The Way of the Cycling Disciple"* by the Velominati Keepers of the Cog was published. This is a book that did for cycling, what was needed for triathlon. It put into writing what was accepted by cyclists as the "rules." *"The Rules,"* however, did more than delineate what was required to be a true cyclist. It also clearly conveyed the inherent snobbery of cyclists, their disdain for all other people in general, and for triathletes in particular.

Neither *"The Laws of Triathlon"* nor a good rebuttal to *"The Rules"* has appeared on the scene. As the subjects overlap, this book attempts to address them both. The challenge was to provide enough basic information as background for the "Law," while still catering to the short attention span of cyclists. As such a "Law" starts with a brief and simplistic explanation for the benefit of cyclists. More detail is then given for interested triathletes.

Law #0.6 is the most important "Law of Triathlon" in general and long distance triathlons in particular. It is also a pretty good mantra for life overall. **Law #0.6** certainly applied to the making of this book...although movement was at times microscopic.

Not all triathletes follow all the "Laws" all the time. Most citizens break the laws of their country every day even if it is just by a couple of MPH. Politicians are in a law breaking world of their own. Laws develop over time. So, if you are a grizzled veteran of the swim-bike-run, it is my hope that you will enjoy the "Laws," and sagely nod, occasionally smile as you read them. Hope being what it is, as you come across a "Law" that you take issue with - please let us know - the same for omissions of "Laws."

While it would seem intuitive to divide the "Laws" into three groups, most triathletes know that nutrition (especially for long course races) is the fourth discipline. For many of us, it is actually the hardest one to figure out. Nutrition definitely has some of nature's laws, which if broken, are flirting with disaster. There is also a final fifth section of the "Laws" that helps define our sport as a whole.

All cultures have an abundance of understood traditions. Triathlon is no exception. The "Laws" include some of these accepted practices and thus, *"The Laws of Triathlon"* is not to be confused with the official race rules. These can be found at www.ironman.com. Please note that the official rules are subject to change. Check the website for the most up-to-date information.

For the majority of the "Laws" a violation will not result in a visit to the penalty tent nor a disqualification (DQ). Public shaming is another matter altogether. As with other cultures, many of the "Laws" are not readily available in some legal document. Immersing oneself in a new culture - understanding and acceptance - requires effort, study and a certain amount of trial and error. As there are often subtle nuances in cultures -

so it is with triathlon. Hopefully *"The Laws of Triathlon"* will eliminate some trial and error.

If you are considering your first tri, or trying to get into Hawaii, hopefully this book will help make a few steps of your journey more enjoyable. May it shorten your learning curve while reducing your public shaming en route. - Volker

Triathlon is a fascinating sport. It challenges you, it changes you and eventually it helps to define you. It can be done with the utmost compulsion or it can be a social endeavor done for the fun of it. My point can be proven by merely spectating at a triathlon. You will see all shapes and sizes; all ages; all genders; all types - those that you would expect and those you would never imagine capable. But as it is so adequately named - triathlon is something that opens the door for anyone to give it a "tri."

One of the most amazing things I have found about a long distance triathlon is not only the distance you will cover, the amount of money, sweat, tears and hours that you will devout to it, but the fact that as long as you have a valid credit card and an up-to-date USAT card, you can sign up for any of them. You do not have to prove that you can swim/bike/run the distance. In fact, you don't have to prove you can swim, bike or run at all. They don't even require proof that you have ever finished a triathlon of any distance.

With that in mind, if you or a loved one finds that they have suddenly committed themselves to the fate of a long course triathlon we hope that the "Laws" can help make a rash decision a memorable journey that ends in the ultimate accomplishment of "You Are An Ironman®."

This is our compilation of "accepted" ways of triathlon to help direct newbies, guide those who are overwhelmed and entertain seasoned triathletes.

*As mentioned by Volker, the most important law of triathlon is **Law #0.6**, so let's get to it. - Robyn*

#0.6 - KMF: Keep Moving Forward.

This is the Ironman® mantra. It's the only way to finish. It's the most important law.

It was Julia Moss's execution of this law in February 1982 that introduced the general population to Ironman®. Moss was a college student who was doing the Ironman World Championship, in part, to gather research for her exercise physiology thesis. As she moved towards the finish line on Ali'i Drive in first place she was severely fatigued and dehydrated. She staggered and fell to the ground, just yards from the *finish line. She got up and staggered some more...then fell again. Once again she got up, staggered and fell. Eventually, she began to crawl towards the finish line. ABC's Wide World of Sports featured the whole thing; Moss's determination inspired millions and created the IRONMAN® theme that, "Anything is Possible®." But you do have to follow **Law #0.6: KMF**.*

In the sport of triathlon the phrase "Just Keep Moving Forward" can be attributed to the blogger and writer, Meredith Atwood. Meredith is better known as "Swim Bike Mom" as her online personality at SwimBikeMom.com, and has helped countless individuals enter (and stay) in the sport of triathlon through her website, writing and involvement in the sport. Her book, "Triathlon for the Every Woman", is one of the most popular triathlon books on the market. She coined and trademarked the phrase "Just Keep Moving Forward" as a way to live everyday life, but also as a way to get through the training and races. "When the training and racing get tough, putting one foot in front of the other is of utmost importance," Meredith says. "That and keeping your sense of humor, always. This sport is full of ups and downs. While you may not move in a precisely linear motion forward, as long as you are using forward momentum (no matter how slow and steady) at all times, the cumulative result will really surprise you."

When I did my first triathlon in 1992, I had not heard of **KMF**. Yet, it is the essence of my years of training and racing. Gandhi said, "The tiger doesn't change his stripes between work and home" (or something to that effect). **KMF** spills over into daily living. Inevitably bad things happen. In the darkest hours, survival is one step at a time, sometimes just making it through the next minute. We all share life's final destination. Life is about the journey and what we make of it. Triathlon instills **KMF** as a habit. As a result, we get the most out of our journeys. Who knows where **KMF** will lead? Just **KMF** out the door.

"If you can't fly, then run,
If you can't run, then walk,
If you can't walk, then crawl,
But whatever you do,
You have to keep moving forward."

- Martin Luther King, Jr

The Swim

#0.6 - Sink or swim. Sinking is not considered a forward motion.

Walking underwater will only get you a limited distance (Jimmy's rule, learned from personal experience). Do not stop and tread water in the middle of the pack - a*nd definitely not in the front of the pack.*

Law #0.6, unless you want to have others swim over top of you so that you can experience near drowning firsthand. *It does not have to be pretty, but you do need to be in motion of some sort - breast stroke, back stroke, double wheel back stroke, or doggy-paddle, whatever it takes.* If you truly need to tread water, try to get to the side of the pack. Better still, start at the back of the pack if you anticipate possible issues. You cannot, however, advance while holding onto the lifeboat (one time **Law #0.6** is in timeout).

#1 - You are a triathlete, not a cyclist.

Cyclists can't swim. However, when they brave the transition to becoming a triathlete, their cycling kick is quite endearing.

If you have a cyclist friend doing their first triathlon, make sure you start in front of them.

#2 - Wear a swim suit under your wetsuit...and tie the draw string.

There has been more than one volunteer wetsuit stripper at a triathlon that got an unwelcome surprise. You are wearing the wetsuit because the water is cold - think shrinkage.

#3 - A triathlon cannot be won on the swim, but it certainly can be lost (drowning will do that for you).

The start of any race includes all the pre-race jitters and adrenaline overload. Not too much harm if you go out a little fast on the run...different story on the swim. Every larger race has people drop out early in the swim...even people who can swim the distance, who have trained to swim the distance.

For many years, the Memphis in May Triathlon's swim took place in the lake at Millington. It has a time trial start format.

For some reason - old guys go last. This meant that Gwin and I had hours to pass before our start. We would watch the race from a dock that was about 150 yards along the course. The relay swimmers were first and started en mass. There were always two or three who made it to the dock and stopped - completely out of breath and sure they were about to drown. Most of the time we successfully coaxed them to relax and then encouraged them to continue swimming. I say most - one time this big guy swam about ten more strokes and then returned to the dock - he got out of the water and told us, "Go F yourself - who do you think you are?"

If you do decide to get out mid-swim, make sure you immediately turn in your timing chip. In 2014, at the USAT National Championship in Milwaukee, after entering the water, a "gentleman" (probably a cyclist) decided that he needed a latte. He climbed out of the swim off to one side and proceeded to a nearby café. Meanwhile race officials were closely monitoring the number of people going in versus the number of people coming out of the water. When they realized this "gentleman" had not exited the swim they delayed the next wave of swimmers for several hours to fruitlessly search the waters. It didn't bother me, because I was already on my way, but it did throw a curve ball for those who had to wait it out. Some had already taken their pre-race fuel and didn't have any extra on them. My guess is those triathletes did not refer to him as a "gentleman."

#4 - If everyone else is swimming into you - you are the one who cannot swim straight.

You are also annoying everyone else, to say the least. With practice it is possible to learn to swim in a straight line. Even if swimming on the diagonal defines your swim - just sight on the people on either side of you and swim parallel to them.

If you happen to have the misfortune of swimming next to a "crooked swimmer," resist the urge to get into a war on the swim. There is contact on most swims. Don't try to push back, just keep swimming. Bodies bounce off each other in the water and it takes the least amount of energy to just let it happen. As soon as you try to push back you are wasting energy needed for the bike and run. The guy beside you is trying to get to his bike, just like you.

Plus, if the water is shallow you may get more than you bargained for. During the last 50 yards of a triathlon swim, I was aiming for the exit ramp and must have had a nice line because the person next to me kept bumping into me (no, I was not the "crooked swimmer"). I tried some gentle persuasion with my elbow, but when that didn't work it became "rather" more forceful. Imagine my surprise when this person stood up in the shallow water, took both hands and totally dunked me. I quickly found a new sight line focusing on the very far side of the ramp.

#5 - Hands off.

The swim is draft legal - but don't touch. One tap of a person's feet may be acceptable as accidental. However, "once a philosopher, twice a pervert."

Done right drafting can improve your time by over 10% and you use less energy. However, the person you are drafting usually doesn't care to help you in this way - so don't rub it in by touching their feet. Once might be forgivable as an accident. More often than that be prepared for an unexpected hard connecting kick. Save the foot massage for post-race.

#6 - Yes, it is OK to pee during the swim. No, it will not turn the water purple.

Remember to pee during the swim just before exiting the water. It's one less thing to worry about on the bike and certainly easier than peeing on the bike.

The other good time to pee is when a guy is drafting off you and keeps hitting your feet. He won't notice the brief rise in water temp - but there will be a certain psychological benefit for you.

Resist the urge to pee in your wetsuit before you enter the water. If it is a chillier morning and you are waiting in line for the race to start, the temptation to pee while in the cover of your wetsuit may be great, but beware the possibility of a delayed start. The person next to you may not notice the slight dripping of steamy liquid puddling underneath you as you each quickly jump in the water. However, if the start is delayed the mistiming of your decision may not be so easily disguised.

#7 - Trust in God but tie your camel. Sight for yourself.

No matter how great the draft or how straight your neighbor seems to be swimming - look for yourself, regularly. In one of my earlier tris, I was merrily swimming and sighting to my right on my neighbor who was swimming exactly the same speed as me. Unfortunately, he was sighting to his left on me. We were practically on the (wrong) shore of the lake before we finally realized our error.

He was probably a cyclist.

#8 - Wetsuit - Don't leave home without it.

Nashville's Music City Triathlon is in July, usually the pavement is melting. In 2013, the swim was wetsuit legal and many were caught without. Now I usually keep my wetsuit well-hidden for southern summer races. It stays secretly tucked behind the truck seat. In 2015, we headed out to that same Music City Tri. Fred (my son in law) gave me a ton of grief when he spied my wetsuit in the back of the truck. The temperature had been in the 90's every day for the last month. The water temperature for our open water lake swims was 85 degrees. Race morning the water temperature was a miraculous 72 degrees and the current in the Cumberland River had doubled overnight (amazing what happens when the upstream dam gets opened just in time for a race). At least Fred had the good grace to get my wetsuit from the truck, as he had also covertly brought his along. Only a handful of people had a wetsuit that day and most of them seemed to be on the experienced (i.e. older) side.

#9 - You do not swim as fast as you think you do - seed yourself realistically.

In a running road race there are often young kids at the very front - ready to sprint off the start line. You just run around them in a few hundred yards. Start at the front of a long course triathlon (with your 1:20:59 PR swim time) and you will feel like a bobber in a wind storm - expect 1,000 people to swim over top of you.

Seeding yourself in a time trial start - especially in a pool swim - is a little trickier. Most people are overly optimistic about their estimated swim time - so you can fudge a little...just don't grumble if an honest swimmer swims over you. *If you pass others remember times you misjudged your own swim time. Don't be a "triathole."*

#10 - The magic number is 76 (degrees Fahrenheit).

Anything less than that and we can wear our wetsuit - unless you are a pro (the price of being good). So don't pee in the lake until the official temperature has been read. You can usually still wear your wetsuit if it's warmer, but you won't be eligible for awards and you usually have to start in the last wave.

According to USAT rules, for other triathlons outside of Ironman® distances, if the water temperature is less than 78 degrees Fahrenheit you can wear your wetsuit. Once again, check the website for the official rules.

#11 - Goggle straps only break on race morning.

Bring an extra set of goggles. Goggles are not the most resilient piece of tri equipment. Chlorine, salt water, excessive heat (all key features in triathlon training/events) can cause the strap to melt or wear over time. So have an extra pair on hand. If you don't need them, you could earn the eternal gratitude of your fellow forgetful triathlete.

#12 - Cover thy head with protective gear be it latex, silicone or lycra.

Swim Caps - bring one. While most triathlons issue a swim cap, not all of them do, especially some of the smaller races *with a pool swim. Of course, in such situations you do not have to wear a swim cap. However, while the flow of water through your hair may feel liberating, it is not very hydrodynamic and being a triathlete you wear a swim cap. If you do not need it for the swim you may find you need it for other purposes (see **Law #66**).*

Wear a swim cap...when training or racing, especially in open water. Not only do swim caps reduce resistance, they are also a safety feature to help boaters see you on the swim. If you practice in open water you should definitely be wearing a brightly colored cap. Even in a pool you should wear your swim cap. Chances are you will race with a swim cap, so you should train with one.

Speaking of safety, when training in open water there are commercially available buoys that attach with a waist belt. They are highly recommended for any open water swims. Contrary to what one might think they are not annoying. As a bonus, they have a compartment which can hold nutrition (or beer) and can double as a floaty.

#13 - The wetsuit zips up in the back. Yes, it would be easier to zip it in front - but it is not a cycling jersey. Yes, it is acceptable to ask someone to help "zip you up." No, it is not acceptable to ask someone to help "unzip you."

Contrary to popular belief, wetsuits do not shrink during the off season. Also just borrowing your friend's scuba suit is not a great idea...there is a difference.

Your first time in a wetsuit should NOT be race day. There is a fine art in how to put on/zip up your wetsuit. What works best for one person may not be the best for someone else. Here are a few helpful tips, learned from experience:

- *Don't use your nails - wetsuits are quite sensitive.*

- *No slack - in the crotch area or the armpits, you want the suit to be flush to the skin.* Although it is interesting swimming with a big air bubble in there.

- *If zipping yourself up, make sure you use one hand to hold the bottom portion of the suit by the zipper so you don't pop a zipper.*

- *Make sure the top flap of the collar by the zipper is flat to the skin.*

- *Know what you prefer to do with the cord from the zipper. This is to help you zip up/un zip the suit. Some people prefer to tuck it in to the Velcro flap to keep the cord from drifting around while on the swim - it is rather disconcerting to have it brush your hand while swimming, not to mention when it wraps itself around your arm or neck.*

- There are several commercially available lubricants. It is best not to use Vaseline® as it can accelerate deterioration of the wetsuit. Apply the lubricant around the neck - especially in the back - to prevent wet suit hickies. Once out of the water we are ready to leave the swim behind - we don't want annoying reminders by sweat trickling into one of those raw areas on a long hot run. Never mind having to explain that "hickie" to your sweetie when you get home after a "race."

- *When removing the wetsuit, make sure you undo the Velcro first, grab the cord and unzip, pull one arm **all the way out** first (doesn't work to do both arms halfway), pull the other arm all the way out and pull the suit down to your waist. This is usually about as far as the removal gets until you make it to transition. Then, pull it all the way down to the legs, stepping on it to help remove it. Many resort to sitting on the ground or wiggling on the ground like a worm. It is quicker to* *learn to remove it while standing, hence the need for practice.*

- *There are numerous other tricks to help get the suit on. Some people put their foot in a plastic bag to make it slide easier through the wetsuit.* Others spray their body with cooking spray, though I have heard, "I used vegetable oil when wearing my wetsuit. The rest of the race I smelt like dinner and got fantastically sunburned." You could just leave your socks on until you have your lower wetsuit in place. *Once again, the safest bet is to practice and find out what works best for you.*

#14 - You are a triathlete not a swimmer.

At least once in your lifetime enter a swim meet...well, OK, at least watch Olympic swimming.

Marvel at the speeds attainable in the water.

Real swimmers don't even own a wetsuit. They swim the 60 degree English Channel with a little Vaseline® dabbed on their lips. Embrace the differences and don't pretend to be a "swimmer." Swimmers have their own set of rules/laws. As much as I occasionally enjoy a swim I wouldn't want to subject myself to their "code of conduct." Most triathletes' dread of cold water is inversely proportional to that of a true swimmer. Opposite for wet suits.

Training for the Rio Olympics, Michael Phelps cut his swims from 85,000 to 60,000 meters per week. Enough said - we are not swimmers.

#15 - Learn how to jump in feet first. Really??

At the start of the New York long course triathlon I focused on holding my goggles on and just jumped off the barge...along with 2,000 others. Not a good idea. First - you can go a long way down into the water, i.e. to the bottom of the Hudson River...not where you want to stick your feet at the start of a long day. By the time I got unstuck from the muck and started to approach the surface, the next triathlete jumped in and landed right on top of me. Back down I went. For a while I thought I was going to spend my day oscillating between surface and slime.

To jump in correctly - make like a lifeguard. Their goal is to keep their eye on the person they intend to rescue, so they strive to jump in and keep their head above water. As you jump, spread your legs apart front to back (like scissors) and spread your arms out to the side. When you hit the water, bring your legs together and start to kick. At contact with the water, slap the surface with outstretched arms as you bring them to your side. Done properly off the side of the pool, your hair won't even get wet. Even off a boat or higher dock, the sinkage will be minimal. It all sounds kind of picky and silly - until you have your feet mired in the bottom of the Hudson.

As always, do not try this for the first time during a race. Waiting to jump off the RMS Segwun steamer at the start of the Gravenhurst Triathlon, my friend asked if I jump in holding onto my goggles. I explained the "life guard water entry" to her. Unfortunately, the jump was over eight feet down. Marilyn's back leg hyperextended when she hit the water. For the next month I got weekly quad "selfies" featuring a resolving hematoma that involved her entire leg. It took even longer to finally get our relationship back on speaking terms.

#16 - Swim practice is more important than swim training.

Either way, you have to get in the water. Recently, a friend who is a very fast cyclist and runner entered his first tri. He finished the swim #219 out of #220 entrants. He commented that he couldn't understand his slow swim. After all, he worked for a pool company and spent all day in a pool. Swimming is a technique sport. So, it is important to get good instructions on technique and then practice. If you train and repeat poor technique over and over, you will not get efficient or fast in the swim. Think of it in terms of a golfer or tennis player who trains by hitting the ball repetitively as hard as possible. A good coach or swim camp (such as Total Immersion®) is the place to start...and then you do have to get wet. In practice, it seems to me that no matter how I focus and get lessons...improvement of my swim time is minimal. On the flipside, I feel much more efficient in my swim and my times have not increased with age, as they have with the bike and run.

Years ago, I was competing with a friend who once was a decent collegiate swimmer. For months before our showdown race I swam daily - worked harder on my swim than ever. David hadn't been in the water for the year preceding the race. We came out of the swim 2 and 3 (I was 3). Technique always trumps fitness in the swim.

That being said, it is good to "go the distance" in swim training. Whereas you would probably not run 26.2 miles and usually not bike much over a hundred miles in training - swimming longer does not take a drastic toll on the body. The recovery period after swimming is much shorter and the danger of injury much less. So practice swimming the distance and even jumping on the bike right afterwards (and riding).

Video your swim at least once a year. How you think you swim is all wet compared to the reality. Bad habits slip in over time. Getting the picture will help you focus your swim and drills on corrective practice. When you think you have it mastered, video your swim again. No worries, it's a lifelong project.

#17 - If you are running late for your race, your wave will be the first to start.

For wave starts, your age group will be last to start - unless you are late for the race, when of course it will be first to go. The same holds true for time trial starts.

#18 - Put your elementary school geometry to use (finally!).

Starting on the far edge of a pack does not increase the distance you swim significantly. If the turn buoy is 1,000 meters away and you start 50 meters to the side of the buoy line you add 5 meters to your swim distance. I doubted this myself, so I cleared some mental cobwebs and finally used that high school geometry - the square of the hypotenuse equals the sum of the squares of the other two sides. So, if you start at the edge and aim just past the buoy you will miss the thrashing at the start and at the buoy turn.

Beware when listening to fellow triathletes as they analyze their swim strategies. I am fairly certain that more times than not they are merely trying to get you out of their way.

#19 - Execute a proper buoy turn.

Learn to make a buoy turn. Not that you will use it very often in a race - but it's just cool. When you get even with the buoy do one backstroke with your inside (next to the buoy) arm. It is easy to use that stroke to change your direction by up to 180 degrees and sight while doing so. Then resume your normal stroke pattern.

This is definitely something that needs to be practiced before doing a race! It is a very efficient way to get around a buoy, with the bonus that you look pretty awesome when you pull it off. When you don't get it right the lifeguards will be at your side determined you are the one who will need to be rescued. Hence the need for practice before putting it into play.

#20 - Those who breathe live to swim another race.

Holding your breath longer while swimming does not increase your buoyancy. It does increase your risk for passing out, especially as your adrenaline and heart rate are already in over drive.

Make a conscious effort to slowly let your breath out as you are swimming and then take a nice big breath in. Even if you typically breathe every third stroke, it is okay to breathe every other stroke if needed. The most important thing is to breathe!

Relax. Breathe. You will always swim faster and more efficiently. Early in my daughter's tri career she had a breakthrough swim. She told me afterwards that she panicked early in the swim - so she focused on looking at the clouds and relaxing - and had one of her fastest swims ever. Personally, I must admit that I don't recall ever noticing the sky during a race.

> *"Winning is the most important thing in my life after breathing. Breathing first, winning next."*
>
> *- George Steinbrenner*

#21 - Pace yourself.

Obviously this is important during the bike and run, also. However, only on the swim will people go directly over top of you if you slow down before they do.

It is good idea to practice your pacing in the pool. One way to accomplish this is to mimic the race environment. In other words, start off with a couple of hard 100's to imitate the start of the race, and then settle into a steady pace. Midway through the swim pick up the pace again to simulate going around a buoy, settle back into your steady pace, and then pick it up at the end to simulate the finish. This will help you find your pace and accustom yourself to the need to accelerate at different points during the swim.

#22 - Not all swimming is created equal.

Swimming in the pool is not the same as swimming in open water. Having swum in the lake when you were a kid is not the same as doing an open water swim in a triathlon. Swimming in a lake is not the same as swimming in the ocean. You need to practice appropriately.

I learned this "Law" the hard way. I have swum all my life. I had a pool growing up, swam in lakes, oceans, rivers and the occasional puddle. I have no fear of the water. Before my first open water triathlon swim, I swam in the pool, a lot. I was very comfortable with breathing every third stroke. I even practiced sighting in the pool. My first open water swim was a time trial start, so it was much less nerve wracking than a wave or mass start. I put my head into the murky water and could not see my hand in front of my face. It was completely disorientating and panic inducing. I swam the whole Olympic distance with my head out of the water - a cross between doggy-paddling and breast stroking. At least, I kept with **Law # 0.6** *but it wasn't pretty.*

The Bike

#0.6 - Coasting counts, despite the condescension of cyclists.

#23 - You are a triathlete and not a cyclist.

Recognize the distinction. Until 2014, I always thought of myself as a cyclist. After all, in the last twenty years, I have put more miles on my bikes than my car. My body bears the scars of unfortunate encounters with other cyclists, dogs, squirrels, armadillos and even a police van while climbing Mt.Ventoux. While it is in triathlon that I primarily compete as an age grouper, it is the bike that is my strongest suit and true passion. It is the bike that gets the most training time. It is The Tour, which is religiously followed in person or otherwise.

After Gwin gave me a copy of *"The Rules"* my cycling world came crashing down. There are numerous "Rules" that exclude triathletes from also being cyclists. Indeed, the comment about one of the authors (Jim Thomson) is "Jim rides a lot and hates people." My impression is that he could easily have added, "And triathletes in particular."

Not only have I come to grips with the fact that I am not and never will be a cyclist, I have actually embraced the concept that I am a triathlete. Through this journey of self discovery, I have realized that triathletes have their own set of rules - *"The Laws of Triathlon."* Still *"The Rules"* remains a must read for all who have ridden or ever plan to ride a bike.

Yes, we do have things in common. However, consider *"The Rules,"* and be happy you are a triathlete and celebrate the differences. Some of the significant ones are:

- Cyclists can't swim.
- Cyclists run only when chased or late.
- Cyclists do not have an upper body.
- Cyclists wear their sun glasses with the arms outside of their helmet straps (a left over archaic custom). Triathletes wear them with the arms inside the helmet straps, as they were designed to be worn. Otherwise, we would have to remove the glasses transitioning from bike to run - such precious seconds squandered.
- For the cyclist - it is about the bike. For triathletes, their bike is more like a very well maintained car...yes, we look after our bike - we just get a qualified mechanic for anything more complicated than changing a tire. Time spent working on a bike is better spent swimming, biking or running.
- Triathletes routinely ride with aerobars. Cyclists view aerobars with disdain. They only reluctantly succumb to their assistance during time trials.

- We use our "man satchel" seat bag because we don't need the pump and spare tube on the swim and run - so why carry them in our pocket?
- Triathletes do their race in one day - cyclists need stages on multiple days.
- Triathlon is an individual event. Cycling is a team sport with a team car trailing to pick up the pieces.
- *"The Rules"* call for standard size water bottles only - triathletes are out there solo without a domestique to bring us a refill. So, we use the biggest bottle we can squeeze into the cage and carry our own water.

#24 - Don't be a "triathole."

Don't show your ass, keep it on the saddle, or close to it. Americans, traditionally, do not have a great reputation when it comes to visiting foreign countries...to the point where American backpackers have been known to resort to sewing a Canadian flag on their pack. Remember - "When in Rome..." By all means - triathletes need to venture out and try bike racing and bike group rides. Just take the time to learn and abide by the "Rules." If not, be prepared for the scorn of the cyclists. If it is a race - DO NOT show up with aero bars on your bike and DO wear proper cycling kit (NO trisuits/sleeveless jerseys). If you show up in a Speedo® - you are definitely on your own.

#25 - Find a cycling guru.

Treat him to a couple of quality cold ones after a ride. Have him guide you through your first bike race. As much as there are definitive differences between cyclists and triathletes - I must admit I have some very good friends who are cyclists (they just pretend they don't know me when we are doing a bike race together).

#26 - Follow group ride etiquette.

On a group ride (which is anything more than your solo ride) you are the eyes for everyone behind you. Point out the road trash and potholes. Call out braking - before you brake. Call out any potential hazard - dogs, cars etc. When you are in back, you are the eyes and ears for all in front of you so call out, "Car back!" when appropriate.

#27 - Hold your line.

When someone calls out "On your left" - do NOT look to your left. Scoot your bike more to the right if possible and then check out speedy as they go by. When you turn your head left to look behind you - as a triathlete - your bike will tend to move to the left - directly into the path of the oncoming faster biker.

However, in a bike race, do NOT, call "On your left," while you are in the pack. The only thing that will move in response is a metaphorical rolling of the cyclists' eyes. They will not move over to let you through. Every inch of space will be guarded even more jealously.

#28 - Even YOUR triathlete brain is irreplaceable.

Whenever you are riding your bike wear your helmet. This also goes for biking to the transition before a race or back to your car afterward...or risk a DQ. Don't be that guy trying to bike to transition while carrying a 10 gallon bucket holding all his stuff, including his helmet.

Helmets are made to absorb energy, much of it via cracking. So when you do wreck - invest in a new helmet. Better a shattered helmet than skull.

#29 - Cyclists take nature breaks. Triathletes are racing.

Peeing on the bike - one of the unspoken joys. However, if you do not need to urinate during the bike portion of a long course triathlon, you are not adequately hydrated. *So, get to drinking and peeing!*

As disgusting as it sounds triathletes pee while on their bike. Urine is sterile after all. I usually try and save it for when I have someone shamelessly drafting behind me.

If you see someone peeing on their bike, do not draw attention to it with comments such as, "That's the way to let it all go," or "You must be nicely hydrated." Most of us do not take pleasure in peeing on the bike, but sometimes it is the nature of the beast. You can get a penalty for urinating while on the bike as well as stopping and peeing on the side of the road. Of course one is a little easier to detect by the officials.

*How you relieved yourself and how much relief you felt afterwards does not need to be shared on Facebook or at dinner (see **Law #129**), unless of course you are dining with other triathletes.*

Nonetheless, it is something you might want to keep in mind if you are in charge of picking up your friend's bike after a triathlon *i.e. handle said bike with care and definitely wash your hands afterwards.*

#30 - For a cyclist cleanliness of the bike is next to Godliness.

As a triathlete you should clean your bike after a race (especially if you followed **Law #29**), before a race (especially a bike race) and before taking it to the bike shop for repairs.

Few things will bring out a cyclist's ire more than a dirty bike (probably worse than showing up in a Speedo®). Believe me, even if you think your bike is pristine, it will not even begin to approach the same level of shine as a cyclist's. Even so, when I bring my bike into the shop my friends ask, "When did you last clean this?" I do not admit that I cleaned my bike that morning. However, I do make sure to not reset my bike computer for several days before taking it in - so it always looks like my last ride was over a century.

#31 - No drafting.

Triathletes do not draft during a race. Cyclists cannot ride without drafting.

The exception of course is an ITU race...although hopefully they, too, will one day see the error of their ways. Do not draft - triathlon is an individual sport. Yes, you will see others drafting in a race - and they seem to get away with it. It is bad mojo. You have 15 seconds to complete your pass and 15 seconds to fall back 5 bike lengths when passed. Do not draft. Still, sooner or later most of us will get a drafting penalty - mine was for drafting a garbage truck - I could not resist.

Training with a group, of course, calls for drafting. Yes, misery loves company. On those long rides it is always nice to have someone with you to help pass the time (and block the wind). However, remember that in a race you will not be able to take advantage of someone's wind blockage (hmmm sounds like a constipated fart), so take your turn on the front when riding in a group - don't just sit back on someone's wheel. You may be averaging higher than when you ride solo, but the effort is not an equivalent. A considerable chunk of your bike training should be solo or on the front.

On windy days most of your time will be spent riding into the wind. This is actually true as you go faster with a tailwind and thus spend less time riding down wind.

During a race when you hear a motorcycle and there is a cyclist in your sights either speed up and pass or slow down. Don't hang in the grey zone. It is their job as referees to make sure everyone is bound by the same set of rules. Contrary to popular belief, they are not intentionally out to get you. Though sometimes I wonder if, like cops, they compete to write the most tickets. When you see a cop, you slow down and have an "Oh, sh*t, what am I doing wrong" moment. This is the same reaction you should have during a triathlon when you hear a motorcycle. At least when you hear a motorcycle, your response can be to accelerate.

Often during a race someone will be "sorta" drafting you. Not really right on your wheel, but in the zone. They know what they are doing and often when they hear a motorcycle they will try to finally complete their pass. This is the perfect time for you to be a little passive aggressive and speed up as well (as subtly as possible). Stretch them beyond their allotted 15 seconds and their only option will be to fall back out of your draft zone (5 bike lengths) or get their deserved penalty. Either way, they probably will not catch back up to annoy you.

#32 - Littering will not make you faster.

Don't litter. If it's a race - use the drop zone for your trash. Out for a ride - carry your spent CO_2 canister and gel wrappers back home. Be a good ambassador for the sport.

When I do a long training run it can be a challenge to find a garbage can for my empty water bottles and nutrition wrappers (I live way out in the "boondocks"). However, after my run (and shower and refueling), I go back to my run route and do a trash pickup, while driving, of course. Not only do I pick up my own trash but any other trash I see alongside the road. I figure it is just good karma.

#33 - Do not lock your bike in transition.

Consider that the 2,000 bikes in transition have a value of over $5,000,000. If your bike looks so hot that a thief would choose it - then you are probably a cyclist and not a triathlete. *And the thief is doing you a favor, as to attempt a triathlon as a cyclist could be very ego damaging.*

If you should be so unfortunate to have your bike stolen the day before the race - check around. In 2015, two competitors from Carolina had their bikes stolen before the Escape from Alcatraz triathlon. Local athletes quickly found them loaners. After all, most triathletes have multiple bikes - a trait we share with cyclists... i.e. we still have every bike we ever bought.

#34 - Read *"The Rules."* Then follow SOME of them.

#35 - Bricks build your foundation.

It is good for your legs to experience the feel of running right off the bike. You don't have to run far nor fast, though it is fine to occasionally do a few pick-ups to mimic what your legs will feel like off the bike in a race. Yes, you can make the time to lay bricks several times a week. Even if it is just a 10 minute run, it will help you physically and mentally.

The best time for a brick is after a bike race or time trial. Cyclists may look down their nose at triathletes, but deep down inside they give grudging recognition to "hardcore." *As soon as you are done with your bike race head out for a brick run. It doesn't have to be far and only has to be fast while in view of the other cyclists.* We may not be able to corner at 50 mph or put on a jacket riding downhill, but we can kick it in a time trial and according to their "Rules" they cannot run. So, let your riding/running do the talking.

#36 - Your bike box will be inspected.

The more carefully you pack your bike in the bike box - the greater the chance that it will get thoroughly inspected at the airport.

Let's face it, there is no great way to travel with a bike, unless you are riding it. Several companies will pick up your bike and drop it off at your destination. But that does not guarantee your bike will be quite the same or that you won't have a tedious wait in line before and after a race. If you invest in a bike box, you have the hassle of trying to fit it into a rental car and hauling it around airports. However, if you do pack your bike - plan on the case being opened and finding the little "notification of inspection" letter. So don't put small or loose parts (like your bike computer) in the box and remember to remove the CO_2 cartridges. Finally, be thankful that your sport is not pentathlon where you would have to carry a horse saddle and fencing apparel as well.

#37 - Is the bike OK?

There are only two kinds of triathletes (and cyclists) - those that have fallen while riding and those that will. Sooner or later it comes with the territory. So, when it happens to you, remember to check your bike for injuries first. It's what the others will be most concerned about. Then be thankful you were wearing your helmet - at least you will be able to remember the wreck.

#38 - Tighten your skewers - EVERY TIME.

Make it a habit to tighten the skewers every time you put the wheel on. Don't plan to tighten them later. Don't just set the wheel in there because you know that tomorrow you are taking it right back off to return it to your car rack for the trip. If it is on the bike it needs to be ready to ride. Forget one time and have your front wheel come off while riding and you will become an ardent believer in this "Law" - trust me.

Additionally, if you think your front wheel is loose - stop to check it. Do not check it while riding. There are triathletes out there who noticed their front wheel seemed loose while riding and pulled up on their bars to check it. Yes, the wheel was loose. Yes, it came off. Yes, their ride for the day was over. The bike was OK though.

#39 - Listen to your bike.

When you suddenly hear a click-click-click every time your wheel turns - stop immediately - and pull the tack/wire out of your tire. There is a small window of opportunity before your tube is punctured. Sadly, there is a small minority of people out there with sun burnt necks that resent their road being blocked by bikes once a year during a race. When your wheel picks up a strewn carpet tack, I have noticed it makes this very distinctive click-click-click sound.

#40 - Let sleeping dogs lie - unless they are on the road.

Some of the back roads don't get a lot of traffic. The best place for animals to catch a few zzz's or rays seems to be in the middle of the road. Just like their owners - our canine best friends do not listen for, or expect a biker. If you surprise them - they will move. Three of the four directions they choose are bad news for you. This happened at the Tour de Paws - a ride raising money for dogs, of course. The blissfully snoozing dog startled - right into the spokes of the lead rider's front wheel. The bike was OK, though.

If you are attacked and suddenly find a pit bull with their teeth embedded in your calf - keep pedaling. I have found it takes about three thump-thump pedal revolutions to persuade him to loosen that grip. Be prepared for the responding officer's concern as they note with a shrug - "Dogs chase bikes - that is what they do."

So give those slumbering dogs an early shout out - or bark - from a safe distance. If they end up chasing you remember the breaking point seems to be 28 MPH. *You can count it as an interval.*

#41 - Bike vs car - car wins - ALWAYS.

Even during a race. Bike not OK.

#42 - Shave those legs - or don't.

Clip a few seconds off your time? Maybe if you are the wooly mammoth. Concerned about fitting in - go for it. Prone to road rash - absolutely stay smooth. Although some races are won by a hair, I doubt that sheared legs were ever the determining factor. Shaving the eyebrows will just make you look even weirder - although there is probably a study out there debating the merits of aero dynamics vs sweat induced visual challenges. As a guy I personally think the time spent pruning legs is better utilized training, eating, sleeping, having a beer or especially rubbing legs with someone the general population expects to be barbered below the waist.

As a female, I recommend you shave those legs. We can reap the aerodynamic benefits without the backlash from friends and family. Of course, if shaving your legs is not your thing, even though you are a female, feel free to exercise your right to freedom of choice. As triathletes, we understand and appreciate each individual's decision. Plus, if the aerodynamic advantages are true I could potentially move up a position in overall women if I race you and you choose to remain unshaved.

#43 - No upside down bikes.

Never, ever turn your bike upside down to fix a flat or replace a chain that fell off. Usually you can get the chain back on while pedaling - just shift in the direction you want the chain to go and continue to pedal softly. Actually - you should never turn your bike upside down ever - it's like telling the world: I know nothing about biking.

#44 - Be self-sufficient.

Carry supplies to fix a flat on your bike. No, it does not add enough weight to slow you down. If you truly worry about that - eat one less donut. Those supplies can easily make the difference between finishing a long course triathlon or not.

A $20 bill also belongs in your bike bag. For a longer tri or run it is similarly not a bad idea to pin a $20 inside a pocket of your trisuit *or put it in your race belt*. Rarely helpful on the swim, but otherwise, you never know when you might bonk, need a beer - or come across a fantastic yard sale. It's also useful, as a last result, to keep a tube from bulging out through a ruined tire after a flat.

#45 - Be one with the bike - be a smooth operator.

Be smooth when you transition to a standing position on the pedals while going uphill. Remember the guy behind you may be in their aero bars or closely drafting. With a little practice you can keep the bike from lurching back. Conversely be aware that the person you are riding behind may come back in your direction when they stand up on the pedals. When wheels touch - the guy in back bites the pavement.

#46 - Remember the roof rack.

I know numerous people (including yours truly) who drove into their garage only to hear/feel that "butt drawing" metal screech. All it takes is coming home late, tired or overly rehydrated. If this happens to you - check your bike carefully. A friend thought his mountain bike was OK. It wasn't until half way through his next ride that he discovered (dramatically) that the front fork was cracked.

#47 - Get a professional bike fit.

Preferably at the beginning of tri season (see **Law #100**). *There is a big difference from sitting on the bike and saying, "Ya, I think that feels good," and actually having a trained professional fit you to the bike. There are different levels of bike fitting. Typically, when you buy a bike from a bike shop they will fit you. However, you can also pay a little more money and get a professional fit. They will analyze your limitations and set the bike up not just how it should be but how it should be for **you** as an **individual**. Let's face it we are all different, with different ranges of motion and flexibility. If you are training for a long course triathlon you will be on your bike for many hours - you want the optimum set up.* Nothing like too much pressure on your hamstrings for 112 miles then getting off the bike and feeling *(and looking)* like Frankenstein doing his first marathon.

#48 - Don't pass half ass.

Pass with authority. When it is time to pass someone, especially someone in your age group, do not do it half-heartedly. Kick it hard and put on a poker faced little smile. You are feeling no pain and it looks way too hard to try and grab your wheel. No drafting invitation extended.

#49 - Know your gears - and use them.

Those big cogs on the back (and the little one on the front) are there for a reason. Use them!

Yes, we all love to mash out the harder gears and laugh at those who need their granny gears, *but at the end of the day you don't get an award for being in the hardest gear for the whole race. It is amazing how much it can save your legs, something that is especially important for a long course triathlon. Professional Australian triathlete (two time winner of Ironman World Championship), Chris McCormack agrees, "Triathletes like to grunt - they want to grind a big gear but this primarily saps your strength. An easier gear for the first one third of the race will help you finish strong for the last two thirds of the race."*

Push the bigger gears during training early in the season - especially up hills. It will help build leg strength. However, as the season progresses ignore the peer pressure during a group ride to mash those big ones. It is best to train as you would race - higher cadence, easier gear. Your run will be happier and faster.

#50 - If you want to make it rain - wash your bike.

The Run

#0.6 - One foot in front of the other, whatever it takes.

While it applies to all aspects of the race - **Law #0.6** is especially the mantra of the run. Everyone encounters rough patches, follow **Law #0.6** and this too shall pass. During Ironman Louisville at mile 6 of the run I started upchucking. Having had this pleasant experience at other races, I shifted to my survival mode - keep walking, pour as much water as you can over yourself at each aid station, then start drinking minuscule amounts while trying a chip or pretzel...hold out for the chicken broth...try and see how many synonyms one can come up with for emesis. It was 6:00 pm and I had 6 hours to cover 20 miles...so sub 18 minute mile pace - my specialty.

At mile 7 spewing became contagious as a female competitor in front of me hurled. I asked her if she was OK and she said she needed a medic. Being the concerned physician that I am I asked why? "Because I'm puking." Dumb ass was implied but not stated verbally, so I pressed on for details. Yes, it was her first long distance triathlon and her first episode of vomiting. "Can you walk a few steps with me?" And so it went. She wanted to know the time and I told her 6:30p.m. She again gave me the "you dumb ass look" until I explained the race time didn't matter, only how much time until midnight. She was an accomplished marathoner, with several Boston's under her belt. The idea of 18 minute miles being good was incomprehensible. Yet, as the miles and hours passed according to our schedule, her despondency was replaced with cautious optimism. We both finished with a very comfortable 15 minute cushion at 11:45 p.m.

#51 - When the finish line is in sight it is time to run (again).

No matter how bad you felt earlier. No matter how slow and painful that run might be. You have to run across the finish and try to smile (okay that may be asking a bit much, so at least run)...they take your picture as you cross you know...

While running to the finish line, remember to respect your fellow finisher. Unless you are truly battling it out for a Kona slot - leave the person in front of you a few yards of space at the finish. Most people only complete one or two long course triathlons in their life - and that finisher's picture is important to them. Pick something else to photo bomb.

For those of you finishing after sunset - remember to flip those sunglasses up. And resist the urge to look at your watch (no matter what time of day it is). Don't worry they will let you know what your race time is (remember the watch is not the dictator of your finishing time the race officials are). Smile.

#52 - Toilet paper - urges hit at the worst of times.

Carry some toilet paper in a baggie on your long runs and bike rides...you will need it when you least expect it. Bringing it with you on the swim is optional.

It is not really necessary during your race, but it is a good thing to have beforehand. It is amazing how quickly those porta potties run out of toilet paper.

#53 - Stretch after every run.

If you don't believe in stretching - try stretching only your left quads, hams, and calves after a long run. Then walk around and notice how much your right leg is pouting. It may seem tedious, but you can make it a habit. It is a routine that your body will thank you for. When you don't feel like spending the extra 10 minutes to stretch just think about how you will feel when you have to miss out on 10 weeks of training or a race due to an injury.

There are many ways you can enhance this stretching session - foam rollers, tennis balls, other massage tools can all help you work out some of those tight, sore spots. "Ready to Run" by Kelly Starrett and "Roll Model" by Jill Miller are a few of the books (there are many out there) that break down some different ways you can stretch and roll away some of the tension spots in your body. Think self-massage.

54 - Railings are meant to be used.

When running upstairs grab the railing and help pull yourself up.

Your arms may be sore from the swim, but they can still help out on the run. It will assist you up the stairs twice as fast, with no extra strain on the quads. Also, try using your hamstrings and push up from your heels when racing up steps. Going up that sand ladder, your quads will thank you even more, maybe even recover a bit.

Yes, in some triathlons there are stairs - best to read your course description and be prepared.

#55 - Race number on the front.

Your race number goes on the front and usually is only compulsory during the run. Use a race belt and put it on while you are running out of transition. Pin it on to your shirt before the race at your own risk. It will provide a nice, distracting challenge when the pin pops open under your wet suit mid swim. Wear it on the bike and annoy everyone else with its incessant flapping in the wind until it finally tears off. Make your life easier and wear it on the front during the run.

In a long course triathlon, the bibs typically have your first name printed on them. This is really nice because spectators get to cheer you on by name. It can be disarming as usually you are a little delirious when you get to the run, but all the same it is helpful. So wear that bib on the front. So that is how all those people knew me?

#56 - Don't judge a book by its cover.

Just because the person running by you looks like they haven't had a piece of chocolate in 10 years, does not mean they are a faster, better runner than you. Don't let someone else's physique mentally do you in (there are enough challenges while running without that). On the other hand, just because someone is not built like a runner does not mean you should use up the last ounce of energy you have to pass them. That is one of the greatest things about this sport. There are people of all shapes and sizes and it is fair game to all of us.

#57 - "But my Garmin says" - good luck with that.

Your Garmin will never sway the race official to change your race time on the run (or bike/swim for that matter). Use it, but watch the mile markers. Even if "according to your Garmin" the finish was actually two tenths of a mile back, the clock will tick until you cross the line.

The advances in technology are amazing and have some definite advantages. Use the Garmin to help judge your pace, monitor your heart rate, and keep an eye on the general amount of miles you have covered but watch those mile markers. The finish line has the final say.

#58 - Accelerate - it is good for your psyche.

There is a time and place to accelerate beyond going down a hill or at the finish line.

Corners are for accelerating. This holds true for both the run and bike (maybe even more so). It is a natural reflex to slow down while running around a corner, but certainly not necessary. After all you are not doing 65 mph. So, use the opportunity to gain a few strides and seconds on your competitors. Make it a habit in training so that it is a natural reaction in a race. It is a good strategy and good psychological tactic.

Hill tops are also for accelerating - same reasoning and similarly important on the bike. You finally top the hill and it's a natural reaction to let up. All good. Just postpone the letting up until you have reached full speed going down the other side.

#59 - Your kit matters not.

Cyclists are fastidious about their "kit." They dedicate more than one "Rule" to the details. Triathletes are not. You do see some triathletes perfectly color/style coordinated head to toe. However, most veterans seem to studiously mix and match. It's not such a big deal as it is for cyclists. It is about how fast and how long you can go. That you are decked out in perfect purple and gold has little to do with finishing that 26.2 miles, let alone the whole 140.6.

Of course, there is no "law" against looking good, or trying to. It is one facet that you have a bit of control over when it comes to a long course triathlon...might make that "Lookin' good" almost believable.

One thing is certain when choosing your kit, make sure those tri shorts are not "well worn" aka see through. If you are uncertain wear them on a bike ride with a female rider. Let her draft you for part of the ride. She will let you know, either by direct comment or via pictures of your visible rear.

#60 - Knees - can't run without them.

The run is most likely the first to cause an injury. Often the knees are the first to go. Swimming and biking usually do not extract the same toll on the body.

However, not all is lost. There are typically ways you can deal with the injury. If the medial (inner) cartilage of your left knee gives out – run on the right shoulder of the road as much as possible. This serves the same purpose as the knee brace (keeping pressure off the medial side) and does it more effectively and comfortably. The opposite of course holds true for the right knee. If both pegs have given out you are SOL and might as well just run down the middle of the highway.

To help prevent wear and tear, spend equal time going clockwise and counter clockwise at the track.

#61 - Form an alliance at your own risk.

A long course triathlon makes for a long day and socializing during the swim is not recommended. However, it is quite cool and makes a race memorable to start up a conversation on the run/walk/survival shuffle with someone moving at your pace. Just be aware that it might be better to call it off at some point. Go too hard early in the run in order to keep up and you jeopardize your nutrition or blow up. Alternatively sharing misery with a fellow triathlete makes it harder to pick up that pace, when you should and are capable. But hey - if he/she is really cute - get your priorities straight. *But do note that outsprinting them at the end will probably nix any chances of getting their phone number after the race. Especially if you are female and they are male.*

The Transition

#0.6 - Set up your transition and then move on.

Head on to somewhere you can focus on the race (like the porta potty). Have a plan - write it down. Chinese proverb: "The faintest ink is better than the best memory." Make a list. Add to it after races where you forgot something. A good transition starts long before you enter the bike corral...your snazzy aero helmet won't do you any good if you left it on the shelf back home. Keep a list of essentials in your tri bag and remember to use the list.

It's a good exercise to visualize your race/transition and pack accordingly. Apparently, I don't wear a race belt during my visualizations, as I have had to borrow one twice this year already.

If you do forget something, do not give up. After finishing the swim at the Gulf Coast Half, a guy in my row of the transition realized that he had forgotten his bike shoes in his hotel room. He ran up to his room after the swim - didn't have a key - found housekeeping to let him in - eventually made it out on the bike - and of course, still beat me. *In fact most forgotten items can be bought or borrowed. However, it is a lot cheaper and less stressful if you pack your own stuff.*

A list is particularly helpful for the morning of a long course triathlon. Create the list weeks in advance and add to it until it's perfect. Include every detail, which also means nutrition. Use the list. Then, when you are going through that hour wait prior to race start, you can focus on your race. Every time you start to think - did I remember my second water bottle, pump my tires, race number etc...you know it's done. There is enough adrenaline and anxiety race morning, no need to worry about forgetting something.

OK, if it wasn't on your list and you cannot stop obsessing - go check. Don't waste energy worrying about it. Just remember to add it to your list for the next race. Check and **Law #0.6**.

#62 - Putting on socks slows you down in a race...but not as much as blisters.

It is OK to leave socks off if you have trained without them. Otherwise, blisters will slow you down a whole lot more than the 20 seconds it takes to put on socks. Set up a sock in each shoe - don't leave them rolled up in a ball. If your friend really struggles with his transition time - give him some socks for Christmas - labeled right and left.

If you are looking to speed up your time, you should definitely have some form of quick laces on your shoes. There are all kinds of elastic styled laces that make slipping your shoes on (while still keeping them tight) a lot easier.

Just don't wear your socks on the swim.

#63 - Remember your transition spot.

At least don't totally embarrass yourself by calling over officials and telling them someone stole your bike...when it is just one row over. Of course if you swim really slowly, your lonely bike will be easy enough to find. *However, when you come back from the bike portion of the race you are in danger of all the rows being filled with bikes, so you still need to know your spot. Even if you are a cyclist chances are there will be triathletes who swam a LOT faster than you and will finish the bike portion before you.*

Remembering your spot becomes even more challenging with age. My friend Tomas, who is in his 70's, was shaking his head at one of his age group competitors. They couldn't find their bike in transition - before the race. This led to the speculation of having a senile moment while transitioning on the bike, with one shoe on and one off - now let's see - am I finishing the bike and heading out on the run, or did I just come out of the swim to start biking???

Identify the different entrances, exits, gear bag locations, change tents etc. - know which direction the traffic flows. If you haven't done the race before, ask a volunteer or fellow racer. It is very distracting (to your race plan, as well as others) if you are a guy heading into the female change tent at a long course triathlon.

#64 - All long course gear bags look alike - mark yours (for the transition).

It's amazing how hard it can be to read those numbers when you are anoxic. I tie a piece of orange tape to mine...makes the bag feel special, too.

There are lots of volunteers at long course events. However, they are not always quick when getting your transition bag. You need to make sure you have your bases covered and are not solely relying on a volunteer to help you. They will indeed try to make your transition smoother but you are better off to not take your chances. You need to take care of you. So, know where your transition bag is and make it stand out.

#65 - Rack your bike on the nose of your bike seat, front wheel on the ground.

If transition gear is allowed, place it beside your front wheel. Keep it simple. Be sure you take your bike for a spin after arriving at transition. Check the brakes and go through the gears. Brake pads can shift during transit. If that has happened it's better to find out before the race. *Do a race one time with your brakes locked on and you will definitely appreciate the value in this "Law."* While sorting out your bike, you can save your spot in transition by leaving your towel on the rack.

And, yes, if you are just coming into transition late - respect that towel. It is not your lucky day. That towel is not saving a spot just for you.

For long course triathlons, it is recommended you do this before race morning (as you are not allowed to take your bike out race morning). Take your bike out for a spin the day before the event. Or bike down to transition to check the gears and brakes. This is not something you want to mess with on race morning.

#66 - An old swim cap makes a great bike seat cover.

It keeps the dew off and protects your seat from the rain. *A bicycle seat is not the most comfortable in the world and a soggy bicycle seat is even worse (plus a soggy seat adds weight to your bike).* Just remember to take the swim cap off before the race. Leave the plastic wrap at home - there is no advantage to covering the whole bike (and it's not allowed).

#67 - Put your timing chip on when you first get up in the morning.

Yes, before your trisuit. It's less likely you will walk out your hotel room door without your suit on than your chip.

I will always remember the look of a pro friend James Loaring *(who won Canadian Triathlon Coach of the Year for 2015)* as he was standing at the water's edge with his wave about to start. He bent over and stretched to touch his toes and suddenly was frantically rubbing his ankle...then madly dashing back to transition to find his chip. Even coaches learn from their mistakes.

Put the chip on your left ankle. If you wear it on the right, it might get in the way of your chain on the bike. Also at the end of the race, volunteers are trained to look at the left ankle. Especially for a long distance triathlon, but also if a wetsuit is worn in shorter triathlons, I would recommend using a safety pin on the Velcro strap. It's amazing how you can feel the chip on the swim and how the mind wants to trick you into stopping your swim - just long enough to confirm that the chip is not as loose as it feels.

Without that chip, you don't get an official time. All the hours spent training, saying "no" to social events and the money invested in getting you to race day morning are lost without that chip. Put it on first thing!

#68 - Body marking can be left on no longer than 24 hours.

It is OK to advertise how much you rock and that you did a big sprint tri yesterday. Leave the numbers on more than a day - you are just letting everyone know that you practice poor hygiene. Also, it is not kosher to return from some hedonist beach holiday and mark your body with numbers to mislead fellow travelers.

Sometimes, that body marking is hard to get off - especially, after a long day of racing. The last thing you may want to do is scrub hard on a worn out body. Using a wash cloth covered with shampoo can help (better than soap). Also, rubbing alcohol helps get the fancier "removable tattoo" style numbers off. A strip of clear packing tape applied to a number tattoo will peel it right off. Finally WD 40 also works - but it hasn't made my list yet.

#69 - Bring your own sharpie.

Have your friend mark your numbers and save standing in line. Just double check that they use the correct number. I offered to mark my transition neighbor at a race. When he returned the favor - I ended up with his number marked on me. This might be a good strategy for drafting on the bike - but I'm sure that there is an official rule/penalty involved somehow.

If you are lucky enough to have a "special" number (such as the number of this "Law") expect some comments. Prepare appropriate "spontaneous" retorts.

Most races have you put your age on your calf, too. Usually this is the age you will be turning that year. Doesn't matter if you have not had your birthday, yet, it is your "race" age.

Except for with "temporary tattoo" race numbers, sunscreen should be put on before your number/age (and allowed to dry). If you try rubbing on sunscreen afterwards you will most likely rub off your number in the process.

#70 - Boasting about your fast transition advertises the lack of your race results otherwise.

It usually means you were beat on the swim and you were beat on the bike and you were beat on the run and you were beat in your age group. We won't even mention where you placed in the overall results. Yes, on the rare occasion a race is won or lost during transition. But if you are called out for bragging - you have been warned.

#71 - Learn to run with your bike while guiding it with your right hand on the seat.

It's the only cool way. It's also faster and you won't get hit by the pedal. Plus, it is easier to carry when needed. Speaking of which, carry your bike out of transition (with your right hand under the nose of the seat) when the transition area is muddy or otherwise nasty. The 2014 Memphis in May triathlon was blessed by a lengthy downpour until after the swim start. Transition resembled a freshly plowed field after three days of rain. It was enough to make a cyclist cry to see the number of people who pushed their nice clean shiny bikes through the mud holes. Most contestants and all the pros even carried their running shoes out of transition before putting them on.

#72 - Haste makes waste.

Not only that, it is quite embarrassing when you finally realize that it is YOU that everyone is yelling at, "You forgot your helmet!" as you push your bike to the bike exit. A friend of mine had this cool aero time trial helmet (you know - with that long pointed tail). He, unfortunately, wore it backwards for a race. When he made it back to his hotel room, he put it on backwards to check himself out in the mirror. His words, "I looked like a retarded shark."

In another situation, a friend left his helmet on as he headed out for the run portion of the triathlon. By the time he realized what those funny looks from fellow runners were all about, he was too far in the run, so he left it on. It was a muddy trail run and this individual did slip a few times and would've taken a hard hit to the head had he not been wearing his helmet. Or at least so he claims in justification for his mistake. In most situations it is better to take your time in transition and ensure your helmet makes it off your head before the run.

*To clarify "take your time" does not mean stop for a foot massage and cold beer before heading out on the bike or run. Though in a long course triathlon definitely take as long as you need, just remember **Law #0.6** and keep your eye on your total time so you make it before the cut off.*

#73 - Bring a headlamp to that early morning start...then try not to shine it into the eyes of everyone else.

Most transition areas are lit in some form, but unless you happen to be right under the light it usually does you little good. Also, those porta potties do not have lights and they can be very scary even in broad daylight.

#74 - Do not squeeze your bike into a rack.

Usually bigger races have a designated spot for your bike. However, some just have designated rows for numbers between "x" and "y." Other, smaller races have open racking based on a first come basis. The prime spot is an end position, closest to the exit.

There are people who take their transition position very serious and wake up that hour earlier to ensure they are first in line to get the best position. I must admit, I might be one of them. It is nice to have the extra room and easier to find your bike if it is on the end. So, if you are running late and all the prime positions are taken do not squeeze your bike in near the start of the row. Do not knock other bikes out of the way. Do not mess up the flow of this-side-that-side bike positioning. Put yourself in the free spot in the middle. During the race, while you search for your bike in the sea of gleaming carbon and titanium, make a mental note to get to transition when it opens next time.

#75 - Have your bike tires aired up and ready to race when you put your bike in transition.

The exception might be if the bike will sit all day in the blistering heat. Otherwise in 12 or 14 hours your tire pressure is not going to drop significantly. Tubular tires do tend to soften a little more than clinchers. If the exact pressure stresses you then add a few extra pounds the night before, if you have to put your trusty steed in the corral prior to race day.

The transition zone the morning of a race is a zoo. Organizers do a good job of having mechanics available to pump tires - but do you really want to stand in line to get that done? Most long course triathlon will not allow you to leave your pump in the transition area. Often it is dark and hard to see that little gauge...why stress over it?

On the other hand if you are loading your bike into the back of the truck or van for an all day summer drive home - it doesn't hurt to let a little air out of the tires first. *If you do this for a fellow triathlete, the courteous thing is to let them know you let air out of their tire so that they don't think they have a flat the next time they head out for a ride. It is also not necessary to let ALL the air out.*

#76 - Clip your bike shoes to the pedals, if you wish.

Just do more than wish on race day - practice getting your feet in and out until it is second nature. The best way to do this is to leave your shoes clipped to the bike during training...so you always mount first and then slip your feet in.

During a race many people fumble trying to get their feet into their shoes when mounted. They lose any seconds of advantage they might have gained. Practicing the dismount is equally important.

Consider the transition area before you decide to run barefoot. Ironman Texas has a good transition run on smooth pavement. Unfortunately, it can be well over 100 degrees by midafternoon. It's not easy running a marathon with the soles of your feet completely blistered (trust me).

#77 - Bring "throw away" clothes.

An old pair of sweat pants, long sleeved shirt (we all have a ridiculous amount of race tees), *gloves, socks and an old pair of running shoes* (we all have lots of those, too) *will help make your race morning more comfortable, especially if it is a little chilly outside. Usually for a long course triathlon you are there early and have a couple of hours wait before the start. So, it is nice to not waste energy shivering. Along those lines an old exercise mat or blow up swim raft is also nice to have to sit or lay on while you wait. It will get you off the cold, hard ground and once again just make your morning a little more comfortable. You are going to have lots of uncomfortable moments throughout the day, might as well do what you can to limit them before your event begins.*

Nutrition

Disclaimer: As I am known to my friends as the Donut King, you may wish to take my input for these Nutrition Laws with the proverbial grain of salt.

#0.6 - Experiment for yourself.

Keep discovering nutrition that works for you (and more commonly what doesn't). Nutrition is the fourth discipline of triathlon. For a long course triathlon, mastering nutrition is at least as important as being able to swim, bike, and run. Even the pros struggle with this one. Whatever you do, do not underestimate this discipline. For many it's the most challenging component to figure out. Some of us never really do.

#78 - Every race is different.

Perfect nutrition in one race may feel disastrous the next time out. Similarly, races feel different from even the hardest training. Any given day tune in to how you feel and be flexible with your nutrition plan.

Always have options. Unfortunately that great vanilla cupcake icing flavored gel you took when training may have bilious results on race day. You would rather eat the fruitcake from last Christmas. If your whole bento box is filled with that type of gel, you can try to force it down and hope the icing sticks. Not the best race nutrition strategy. Instead have an assortment of flavors and items that you know work for you. Use your special needs bags for more options.

#79 - Beer is the ideal fluid replacement: post-race.

Though it may be tempting, save it for after the race. In 1999 pro Chuckie Veylupek was DQ'ed from the Ironman World Championship after taking a "few sips" of spectator offered beer.

In an article posted on the ABC website, "Sports Medicine Experts Bust Marathon Training Myths," one of the myths they commented on was "Beer can help relieve aches and pains." According to the article, "beer (in moderation) can in fact act as a muscle relaxer and help diminish the pain of a long run." So, there you have it if it can help act as a muscle relaxer and help you recover after a marathon – imagine what it will do for you after completing a long course triathlon.

#80 - To go longer and be faster - be leaner.

As mentioned in more detail in *Law #110*, an extra 10 pounds is like wearing a coat in the summer. You can still bike and run with it on, but not as fast and the nutrition is much more of a challenge. In other words your nutrition in the months leading up to your long course triathlon is important 24/7, not only while training.

#81 - Homeostasis is the number one law of nutrition.

While not every triathlete is OCD, everyone's body is. Your body insists on maintaining a very narrow ideal range. Whether this is your blood glucose level, sodium, potassium, blood pressure, body temperature or other regulated parameters - your body is exceptionally well designed to maintain a well-controlled steady state.

Homeostasis is like a plateau. For example, if your sodium is between 137 and 145 millimoles per liter (which is like a dozen grains of salt in a pint), you are good to go. You are on the flat even top of the plateau. If it drops to 132 you feel bad - you are on the plateau edge. If there is no corrective action and your sodium drops to 125 you are tumbling down the steep slope. Your body shuts down any way that it can to remove the threat of a further drop in your sodium. You are overcome with nausea and vomiting, you are faint, you have stomach cramps and desperately seek out a porta potty or bush. Your body doesn't care how it stops your insane push to keep moving - it will put a stop to it. This is also known as "the bonk" - one minute you are going great, the next minute you shut down - your blood sugar has dropped that critical 10 points and knocked you off the plateau. Same for body temperature. Your body is amazing - you are out there running in 90 degrees creating all kinds of internal heat - your body temperature stays very close to 98.6...until it runs low on fluids. Dehydrate, overheat and fall off the plateau.

The slope is steep and slippery. Once on it, the climb back up is arduous. You will not go far or fast once off the plateau. Your body does this intentionally. You have threatened the viability of your vital organs (i.e. brain and heart). You have to work for forgiveness and suffer. There is a price you pay for jeopardizing what keeps you alive. At this point one could make a case for not saving a triathlete's brain - after all they are a little crazy to even attempt a long course triathlon. Luckily our body doesn't know any better.

Falling off the plateau of homeostasis affects different people in different ways. Likewise, climbing back up varies based on the kind of insult your body received. A bonk might be cured in 15 - 45 minutes by ingesting some carbs. Overheating might require hours to recover. Lightheaded and nauseated, vomiting anything you dare ingest - forces most of us to either slow down or get dragged to the medical tent. Not listening to what your body is telling you at this point can be fatal. Usually people survive - because your body is so well tuned to self-preservation.

One reason for the nausea and intestinal problems with overheating and dehydration is that the body shunts blood from less important organ systems (i.e. your intestines) to important ones (your brain). Yeah, one would think that would be the other way around. A decrease in the normal blood flow to the gut, results in a decrease of the normal source of energy and a build-up of waste products (think lactic acid). At this point it is too late to pour in fluids. Peristalsis has ceased and the bowel is on strike. Your stomach has little blood flow and is shut down. Fluids slosh around and create discomfort, nausea and vomiting. They will only move one way - back from whence they came, until the crisis is passed. Most of us are forced to slow way down when this happens and do not get going again for hours.

Of course, there are exceptions. Chris Legh, professional triathlete in Ironman Hawaii 2011, pushed through the "abdominal discomfort." As a result, the blood flow to his small intestine shut down completely. As soon as he finished the race he required emergency surgery to remove the bowel that had died. Similar to putting a tight tourniquet around your arm and leaving it on long enough to where it was no longer viable...resulting in amputation.

Yes nutrition, especially for a long course triathlon, is not something to be ignored. You would not swim 2.4 miles without training. Similarly, we need to rehearse our nutrition.

#82 - Small, frequent feedings.

The key to solving the nutrition puzzle includes small but frequent feedings. Seven Bugles® have the same amount of sodium as a salt pill and they taste better (even without the beer).

#83 - Stay tuned to your body.

The warning signs of an impending nutritional crash will be there - train yourself to recognize them.

Out on the bike in the heat - take a look: soaked in sweat - good to go. "Nice and dry" - you are about to slide off the homeostasis plateau. Drink up. Not sure if it's a bonk or early dehydration? Practice a bonk. Upon waking in the morning, wash down two pop tarts with a coke. Wait 15 minutes and head out for a hard run. A few miles into the run your body's insulin surge (to rid the healthy breakfast) will coincide with the need for calories to suddenly fuel your quads. Feel a little weak and sluggish? Have a gel and feel better in 10 minutes. You just went through a mini bonk. When you are out on that 112 mile bike and catch that little feeling creeping in - eat - don't wait until you get to the top of the hill or pass the next guy. Eat or slide off the plateau.

#84 - You are an experiment of one.

While there are volumes of information available pertaining to race day and training nutrition, everyone is different and every race will be different for you. So write it down just like you do your workout. Plan it out just like you do your race. Discover what works best for you. An interesting learning experience is to volunteer at the bike special needs station. People have everything from Cheetos® to sandwiches and can't wait to get to them. Personally, I wish that I could get a fresh corn dog at the half way point of a long course triathlon. For some ideas (semi-serious ones that is) for the Special Needs Bag see the Appendix.

Do what works for you. Just because one person can take 20 plus gels during a long course race and is fine does not mean it will work for you. There are tons of articles and books written about the nutrition side of longer races detailing exactly when you should take in "x" number of calories comprised of so many carbs, etc. You can follow these guidelines to a "t" and still run into gut issues. The best thing to do is practice, practice, practice. Just like you spend hours of training on the swim, bike and run you need to practice your nutrition. Find out what foods work for you whether they be gels, chomps, real food or a combination. The only way you can know what you can and can't tolerate is by trying.

The legendary Bob Babbitt (co-founder of Competitor Magazine and the Challenged Athletes Foundation as well as a USAT and Ironman Hall of Fame inductee) says it best, "Experts are great, but becoming an expert on you is even better." He details one of the classic examples of this "Law" in his book "Never a Bad Day." Chris McCormack (Macca) is a two time winner of the Ironman World Championship in Kona (2007/2010). In his early days of racing, he struggled against the heat in Kona. He worked with physiologists and nutritionists to figure out a strategy to cope with this heat.

In 2005, he was falling off his pace on the way out to the turnaround, Thomas Hellriegel (1996 Ironman World Champion) passed him and suggested that Macca drink some Coke. "I was told to never drink Coke in a race by the nutritionists," Macca says. "I was pretty frustrated and desperate at that point of the race, so I drank a Coke and it was like jet fuel." McCormack had his best time at Kona that day (up until that point). He ran a 2:49 off the bike and finished sixth, his first time in the top ten. Through his own experience (and not any easy time of it) he learned that, no matter what the experts say, for him a little carbonated syrup plus caffeine can actually be a good thing.

As a side note, consider avoiding caffeine before the swim to help keep your jitters down or make sure you train with it and practice taking caffeine before a swim in some smaller races. At race time you do not want to realize that you, 2.4 miles of open water, 2000 other thrashing bodies and caffeine do not mix.

#85 - Prevention is better than treatment - as in all things medical.

Know how many carbs, electrolytes and fluids you will need for your race. Factor in your pace, conditioning and race day conditions including wind, temperature and humidity. Then plan your day accordingly. Some people set their watch to beep every 15 minutes to remind themselves it's time to drink/eat etc.

With all the calorie counting and analyzing of carbs vs. protein, etc. you tend to feel like a scientist, well, a mad scientist that is. But perform poorly in a race or two due to nutrition, after putting in the hours of training and you will be a believer in the need to analyze.

#86 - If homeostasis is the first law of nutrition then water is the numero uno component.

Weigh yourself before and after longer workouts. Learn how far behind you fall in fluid replacement and then do better next time. The weigh-in is more accurate if done in the nude and does not require witnessing. *So, please do it behind closed doors of your own home.*

Hydration becomes even more important as the temperatures climb and even more important if you are on the heavier side. *To quote Macca again, he notes, "As a guy who has spent years trying to master this, and as the biggest ever winner of the Hawaii Ironman (by more than 14 pounds) I can attest that hydration and fluid loss will hurt you more than lack of calories. You need to address your calories but really nail your hydration. Your margin of error here is much smaller than a smaller individual and your drop off is much greater."*

Drink cold fluids if at all possible. They are more readily absorbed and provide the additional benefit of their direct cooling action. On the bike grab water closer to the center of the aid station (closer to the iced bottles). Take 5 extra seconds and add ice to your hand held on the run.

Water poured on your head during the bike or run is almost as beneficial as swallowed in terms of preventing overheating and dehydration. Your gut can only absorb so much and at a finite rate. The extra poured on top of you saves that much sweat and GI stress. Of course, mistakenly dousing yourself with a sports drink is not that cool.

Consider carrying a "hand held" on the run, particularly if you are prone to dehydration or nausea/vomiting. Train with one and they become less of an annoyance. It only takes a few seconds to refill with ice water at the aid stations. Liberal squirts on the head from your hand held will get you through a marathon even if you can't drink anything for miles.

If it is a race during the heat of the summer, you might want to consider having your CamelBak® for the bike portion. Just make sure you train with the CamelBak® and whatever helmet you plan to wear race day. Some of the "tails" of the aero helmets are quite long and create an awkward position when a CamelBak® is worn.

It is interesting to hear stories from people who have experienced dehydration at a race. Typically, they still had water in their water bottles from the bike. If you find yourself low on water and thirsty, drink what you have. Preserving it could be leading you towards disaster. Make sure you stop at the next aid station to refill - even if that means literally stopping your bike.

#87 - You can train your gut.

Actually, you have to train it. Part A of that includes planning how you are going to have access to the six liters of fluid you need to drink during your ride. Part B is actually drinking it.

#88 - Nutrition trumps speed.

If you are dehydrating during a race and don't want to slow for that aid station to grab a water, you better think again. If you are too busy hammering your bike to grab a bite, you better think again. Your body will maintain nutritional needs - and you will slide off the plateau if you try and sacrifice that for the need for speed.

#89 - Sometimes it is better to stop for 5 or 10 minutes.

What? Disobey the **Law #0.6**?!? Think of it as moving forward with the nutrition part of the race. If you have gotten to the point where you know you are about to slide off the plateau, there is a window of opportunity which can only be opened by stopping your bike or run - just long enough to safely get back on the plateau. Ten minutes in the shade of an aid station, drinking what you can, while pouring ice water all over yourself to cool down is not 10 minutes lost. It may mean the difference between finishing or not - being able to keep running or having to resort to the death march. Utilized properly you are still moving forward.

A book about amazing athletic achievements, fascinating science and pure inspiration, "Born to Run" by Christopher McDougall, has an excellent demonstration of this Law via

Scott Jurek. Jurek is a Western States Champ and has been Ultrarunner of the Year. Now ultrarunning is a completely different ballgame compared to doing long course triathlons. I, for one, cannot fathom running for more than 26.2 miles. However, as in all endurance sports some points transfer from one to the other. Such as this "Law."

In "Born to Run" McDougall describes Jurek's experience of the 2005 Badwater Ultramarathon in Death Valley. The temperature was around 200 degrees - the temperature you need to slow roast a prime rib. Jurek was racing this ultramarathon for the first time, it was 35 miles longer than he had ever raced.

At mile 60, Jurek was vomiting and shaky. He wasn't even at the halfway mark and his competitors were so far ahead he couldn't even see them.

As he lay by the side of the road, Jurek had a heart-to-heart with himself noting that it was a hopeless situation. The only way he could win was by "starting all over again" and "pretending like he just woke up from a great night's sleep and that the race hadn't even started yet." He laid there for 10 minutes and then got up and did it. He broke the Badwater course record with a time of 24:36.

I am not saying that by stopping you will then be able to run like Scott Jurek. However, it gives your body a chance to reset and if you can get your mindset into the "start over" position you may surprise yourself.

The most unique "reset" button I have used was discovered quite inadvertently. Participating in a family vacation I allowed my daughter to sign me up for the Disney Dopey Challenge. This is four consecutive days of running (5K, 10K, half marathon and full marathon). I was woefully undertrained (and carrying an extra 40 pounds) with a "long" run of 10 K in the preceding two months. Fortunately, the Disney Challenge can be more of a fun run/experience than a race.

With a Mickey, Donald, Captain Hook or any other famous character every mile - there were lots of excuses to stop for a photo op. Of course, the more famous characters had longer lines with lots of people waiting for pictures. After the first ten miles of the marathon my run had turned into a steady plodding - but forward - motion. As such I stopped wasting energy walking to the front of the line to check out the characters and then retracing steps back to the end of the line for the picture. I just joined every line.

At the 12 mile mark I was seriously questioning my ability to escape the "broom" and finish within the allotted time frame. I joined the end of a longer line. Before I realized the error of my ways, the line swept me on to the Mt. Everest rollercoaster. Sheer terror. I do not typically venture up the third step of a ladder. When driving across any larger bridge my vehicle will not budge from the center lane so that I cannot see over the edge. I do NOT do rollercoasters. Miraculously, I did manage one selfie at the start – without which none of my friends would have believed the story. When I hit the exit I was "reset" and had my fastest two miles of the marathon. With my 8 hour plus finishing time, I managed to finish 815 out of 815 in my age group.

#90 - Salt - if in doubt add more.

It is very difficult to overdo ingestion of sodium chloride. About the only way is to drink the water of an ocean swim or to consume a whole bottle of salt pills at once. Watching one quarter of a football game I can easily consume a big bag of Bugles - 4,030 mg, 170% of the body's total daily sodium needs - not counting what is in the beers. There are consequences of this method of nutrition, but not because of the salt intake.

Athletes do not end up in the medical tent because their sodium is too high - unless it's a result of over concentrated blood due to dehydration.

On the flip side, it is relatively easy to have your sodium drop too low. Dilutional hyponatremia has claimed the life of more than one marathoner. Of course, if you are one of those that finish a hot race looking like a salt lick, you need more NaCl than others. Even if you are not - an extra salt pill won't hurt you. As you can tell my personal preference is to stuff my Bento box with Bugles®. Seven Bugles® are one salt pill and they are easier to grab while tasting better and providing a few carbs as well. Besides, they are made with coconut oil, so at least one ingredient is "good for you."

Potassium and other electrolytes also should not be ignored. However, most foods or commercial electrolyte pills/solutions address these elements just fine.

The one exception to the liberal salt recommendations are for any of you who might have heart failure, hypertension or are on a salt restricted diet. Even then, with exercise you will need to increase your salt intake to allow for what is lost through perspiration.

#91 - Puking is allowed - but never on your own (or someone else's) shoes.

Sometimes a little projectile vomiting is even a welcome relief. It's amazing how little or how much can come out of that shut down gut. During a race, emesis gives you an opportunity to "reset." After a race a good gut evacuation makes room to exchange nasty Gatorade for a refreshing cold beverage. If you somehow vomit on a cyclist's bike, please have someone video the reaction and send me a copy.

#92 - Do not freeze your water bottles.

Chances are they will expand and not fit into your water bottle cage. The bottle will crack and the water will all have leaked out by the time you mount your bike. The water will not melt at all and you will be sucking on an ice cube.

Using an insulated bottle filled with ice cubes and water works much better.

#93 - Aid stations just slow you down - Right!

This is as much fallacy as there will be plenty of porta potties with no lines. Especially a long course triathlon will extract a serious toll if you don't get adequate refueling throughout the day. Nothing wrong and lots right with walking through the aid station.

#94 - When you stop caring eat some chocolate.

Karen Smyers, Ironman World Champion in 1990, 1995 and 1996 gave the following advice at one of her training camps, "If you are running and you feel like you just don't care, if you get really apathetic - you probably need sugar!" In Chrissie Wellington's book "A Life without Limits" she notes that on the bike she takes a bite of chocolate every hour. Of course, since she is only out on the bike for a few hours her chocolate bar probably stays intact. Mine would be one big, ooey, gooey mess, but at least a tasty one.

#95 - Bring extra prerace nutrition.

*Race morning starts early. After getting to the race venue and setting up your transition area you need to top off the caloric reservoir. Always bring some extra gels or bananas. You never know when there will be a delay in the race start or if your buddy forgot their snack and you have to share. The last thing you want to do is to take your prerace gel, then be delayed by an hour or so, starting your race on an empty tank. See **Law #3**.*

#96 - Keep a nutrition log.

At least for longer workouts and training for a long course triathlon, recording things pertinent to your nutrition is as essential as logging your miles, heart rate and power output. Include your pre/post weight. Gain 5 pounds...fewer corn dogs on the bike next time. Was your urine a reluctant, dark, dehydrated dribble or a glorious, copious, clear stream? What amount and type of fluids and nutrition went down well? What did you want to share with your co-riders instead? Did you feel great hammering the initial 60 miles but finish with a survival shuffle 3 mile brick? Were the dogs refusing to leave their shade to chase you on melting pavement? Did you work to average 12 mph into that headwind from hell that changed with every turn? Or was it a cool clear calm day - where you only had time for a one hour workout? What did you try nutrition wise? Did it help or make things worse? What to try different next work out? What did you take in before and after your workout?

Race day rolls around and it is predicted to be sunny, 90% humidity and 85 degrees. It helps to be able to look at your nutrition notes, pick a similar day and say: OK I need to drink 6 bottles of water. Bugles® will work better today than gels or donuts. I'm going out a little slower and hitting every aid station.

*There is no need to share these details on Facebook see **Law #129**.*

General Laws

#0.6 = Rule #5 from "The Rules."

If there seems to be a conflict with other Laws, **Law #0.6** is King.

#97 - Be happy.

Enjoy your race. Embrace your training. The stormiest rides, the gnarliest swims and the genitalia freezing runs will become your most memorable.

There comes a point in every event, where you know, "I've got this." Smile. Allow yourself the luxury of having that feeling sweep over you. Press the save button and forever lock it into your memory. You will want to call on it often - like when it's time for your next training ride in the cold rain or long run in the blistering heat. There is also the flip side unfortunately...there may be a point (especially during a long course triathlon) when you know you will not make it before midnight. Don't beat yourself up - 99% of people never even make it to the starting line. The sun will rise again.

Lew Hollander is an 85 year old triathlete who is a 58-time long course finisher (as of Oct 2015). He has done the Ironman World Championship in Hawaii more than 20 times. In 2014, he decided to drop out of the World Championship as he realized his performance on the bike in the soaring temperatures and the ferocious winds would not leave him enough time to complete the run within the needed time frame. It was the first time he ever had to pull out of a race. What did Hollander do? He did Ironman Florida the next month and qualified again for the Ironman World Championship. We all have our days.

Share the Joy. By participating in triathlons, you are in a small percentage of the population...and in the fitter minority. You spend a lot of time training - often solo efforts. It takes dedication and desire. So take some time outs during the year to celebrate with your tri friends (yes, and cyclist/runner friends, too). Stick around for awards, swap race stories. *Let loose a little and have a drink or two. Some ice cream and/or donuts will not kill you. You work hard for it; allow yourself the pleasure of a reward.*

The days leading up to a long course triathlon are typically stressful. Often, you do not appreciate the venue of the race. So, after the race, stay in town an extra day. The day after Ironman Coeur d'Alene Gwin and I took up residence at a sidewalk table of a corner bar downtown. There was a steady stream of locals who had done the race...nothing like a few beers and a shared long course triathlon to develop instant camaraderie.

98 - Traditions repeat themselves...so develop some good ones.

After the Memphis in May triathlon, we all meet up back home in the hot tub and fill the floating cooler with magnums of champagne. We soak our battered bodies and swap tri stories.

Every year we have a Christmas run for local triathletes and runners (sorry no cyclists, as by definition they can't run – their "rules" not ours). This run is followed by awards commemorating the year's memorable moment for each of us (e.g. see **Law # 72** re wearing your aero helmet backwards). The most coveted and only serious award is the Nutcracker (one of those two foot tall red wooden ones) – awarded to the person who had the most amazing year. The winner gets to sign it and keep it on their mantle for a year. It's a tough one to win. Kirsten was USAT's female amateur athlete of the year and still did not win it...as Bonnie edged her by doing her 50th state marathon that year*.

Personally, I have never won the Nutcracker. After 25 years of trying to qualify for Kona, I finally made it so I thought 2014 would be my "nutcracker" year. However, Gwin had to go and get throat cancer. Even while going through chemo, radiation, a feeding tube and all the other challenges that cancer deals one, Gwin never missed our monthly time trial. He even did a time trial with a fanny pack holding his chemo pump. It's a tough crowd. He couldn't compete in Ironman Florida, which he had signed up for prior to his diagnosis. However, he did travel with us and cheer us on. This in itself created a memorable moment. As we were recuperating in the hot tub the day after the race, several triathletes joined us. Gwin had them going, as he explained that it wasn't a feeding tube, but the latest, greatest way to get nutrition on the bike...you just hook your hydration system to it and you have a steady influx of fluid and nutrition. No need to ever come out of your aero bars. In 2015, Gwin placed third in the 60-64 age group at Florida (without a feeding tube).

*This point is somewhat controversial as she did a 30 mile ultra for Kentucky and counted that as 26.2. I believe it is a "running law" that a marathon is running 26.2 miles and, as such, a long course triathlon or ultra does not count. But we will save that argument for another time.

#99 - Participate in the underwear run, even if commando is your normal default setting.

If you are a cyclist don't be embarrassed by your anatomical short comings - you can at least show off your cycling tan lines.

Back in the day, all the guys wore Speedos® for triathlons, which caused a bit of a reaction from the general populace. Even after trisuits became readily available, there remained some stubborn few (from the old country) who have persisted in this form of exhibitionism. American counterparts gave birth to the underwear run as a form of poking a little fun at triathletes (secretly they just wanted an excuse to showcase their inner Speedo®). So, participate in the tradition. The run is short and co-ed! Enjoy the guys in their whitey tighties or the girls in their Victoria Secret® attire. Personally, as this public display is socially acceptable, I am thankful it hasn't made its way into the work place.

Hmmmmm, "guys in whitey tighties" vs. "girls in their Victoria Secret® attire" - it may not sound appealing for the female population. However, have no fear ladies; there are guys in "whitey tighties" but also those who could be auditioning for a Calvin Klein® ad. Additionally, there may be girls in their Victoria Secret® attire but not all of them are Victoria Secret® models. So don't be afraid to be a part of the liberation.

#100 - Nothing new on days leading up to a race or on the big day itself.

Change, experiment and improvisation are for training. Do not change anything on race day. No new clothes, shoes, food, bike, hat, sun glasses. Sure it may be fine - but really - you couldn't plan enough to try it even once in training? I had trained months for Florida - faithfully wearing my fuel belt with its four max size fluid containers. Race day was hot and I decided to store my running belt in a mini cooler with ice (for the first time). Nice cold drinks to start the mid day run. After all, the fluids would be close to 100 degrees otherwise. It seems a soaked fuel belt stretches. It stretches a lot. It isn't easy to run with it sliding to your knees either. In the end it was a run without a fuel belt.

Nothing new before a race includes dinner the night before or breakfast the morning of a race. Now is not the time to experiment with, "Well, so-and-so always eats Mexican the night before a race and they are fast." Or, "I usually just have a bagel with cream cheese before a hard work out/race, but I think I have time for the hotel breakfast buffet race morning." Sometimes, you will be fine and on the rare occasion you may find a new go-to meal. However, if it does not work in your favor (and it usually does not) you will have a very unhappy gut and unpleasant racing experience.

Nothing new on your bike set up within two weeks of your race start. Yes, replacing the chain and cables that originally came with your 10 year old bike is a good idea. Just do that a month before the race. Chains need adjusting and cables stretch. New tires and tubes are great - just ride on them a few times to make sure they are not defective and properly installed. So, your cyclist guru says you should raise your seat ½ inch. This is not the time to do it.

#101 - "Looking good!" Should set off warning bells in your fried brain.

It definitely should not be taken literally. It's what well-meaning spectators call out as encouragement, when they really mean, "Don't have your cardiac arrest in front of me, please!" *Similarly, "You're almost there!" rarely has any relationship to the actual distance yet to cover. So, don't get your hopes up and don't get frustrated with the innocent soul who is trying to find ways to help you along (even if it is just* so they don't have to witness your collapse).

#102 - When training for a long course triathlon, the days crawl by but months fly.

Typically, you have to sign up a year ahead of time. You will most diligently lay out a training plan that taken day by day is very doable. The problems arise when, "It is still 6 months away and it won't make any difference if I skip my run today." It doesn't take long to get off track and catching up usually means adjusting your goals. Yes, I sense some of you agreeing with this. A training plan is only as good as its implementation. Remember the Irish proverb: "Nodding your head does not row the boat."

#103 - Sh*t happens - to cyclists and triathletes alike - it is how you deal with it during a race that matters.

A long distance triathlon takes most of the day (and for some of us part of the night). How many non-racing days have you had where everything is perfect? Nothing at all goes wrong? Right, that is why they make good bourbon and Happy Hour. Something will not go as planned during your race - you might as well plan on it. Don't let it control you. If nothing else, it will provide a good post-race story, embellish away.

There are lots of books available that explore the mental challenges triathlons pose. One is "Triathlete EQ: A Guide for Emotional Endurance" by Dr. Izzy Justice. It encourages you to create race plans that include detailing all the things that could go wrong and how you plan to overcome those challenges. By having thought about it and "planned" it, you will be able to keep your cool and overcome that problem.

At the 2008 Ironman World Championship, Chrissie Wellington flatted on the bike. The rear tire, of course. She replaced the tube and tire but when she went to inflate it her CO2 cartridges malfunctioned and she was stuck on the side of the road waiting for technical support. She eventually resorted to requesting help from her fellow athletes. Rebekah Keat gave her a cartridge. This time Chrissie got her tire sorted and proceeded to get back into the race. She lost 11 minutes and was more than five minutes behind the lead woman. She managed to pass them all and finish as the World Championship with a 15 minute lead over the second place female. So Sh*t happens, but it is not the end of the race.

#104 - It's okay to have a "Shane Moment."

Shane Eversfield, author of *"Zendurance,"* gave a presentation at a Total Immersion® swim camp I attended about his training for a triple long distance triathlon. That would be 7.2 miles of swimming, 336 miles of biking (around a 2 mile track) and a 78.6 mile run all in one setting. He succeeded (if you can call it that) and finished the event. However, at mile ONE of the swim he stopped swimming. Treading water he asked himself, "What in the f*ck am I doing?" and almost quit. Our group dubbed that a "Shane Moment." Having a "Shane Moment" is part of doing triathlons. To have a "Shane Moment" shortly before doing a long course triathlon is normal. To have one (or more) during a triathlon is a rite of passage. The important part is to remember **Law #0.6.**

#105 - Thank the volunteers.

That doesn't mean mumble something under your breath while you reach for that plastic cup of water (unless that is all you are capable of). Look them in the eye and thank them, genuinely. They are volunteers - meaning they are not getting paid to stand in the heat while encouraging a group of sweaty, stinky, high-strung athletes. They have gotten up just as early as you - if not earlier - and most of them will be out there almost as long as you - if not longer. They don't have the satisfaction of completing a triathlon. The only pleasure they have is knowing that they made a difference for the athletes and let's face it, they do make a difference. So look them in the eye, smile and thank them from the bottom of your heart. Without them it would be a long, lonely road, with a lot more cars to dodge.

#106 - Don't be a sore loser.

When someone beats you, make sure you congratulate them at the finish or up on the podium. This goes for people in your age group, your gender division or even that person who out sprinted you to the finish (there is always a race within a race).

In 2001, while racing Kona, pro Chris Legh, was suffering issues form the effects of pulmonary edema. As a result of coughing up blood, he had to walk a large portion of the run. Eventually he was able to start running again and was jogging his way back to town with a fellow Aussie. Legh recalls, "I figured we'd jog our way in. I just wanted the day over." Well, a hundred yards from the finish, the music and lights jumpstarted Legh's "jogging" buddy and he took off like a bullet. It didn't matter that Legh and his fellow Aussie were nowhere in the same division. In fact, at that point, Legh was three-and-a-half hours behind the winners. Legh still sprinted for the line. It is a common occurrence you will see in many races and will more than likely be subjected to. The two ended up with identical times of 11:43:35 though Legh claims he was ahead by a nose. "I out leaned him," says Legh, laughing. "Through the years of racing, you learn that when things turn *to crap, you simply have to make the best of it." - Taken from "Never a Bad Day" by Bob Babbitt (co-founder of Competitor Magazine and the Challenged Athletes Foundation as well as a USAT and Ironman Hall of Fame inductee).*

#107 - Pass it on.

With enough encouragement, even stubborn cyclists occasionally will see the light and cross over to the tri side.

One of the best things about this sport is sharing the love and passion we have for it. My father was one of the first people in our area to get involved in triathlon. Before he knew it, he had quite a group of (diverse) friends who shared the joys and challenges of triathlons. He eventually got my sister involved and then somehow I was roped into it, as well. It is not just putting in the miles of training or collecting the medals/trophies, it is all the experiences in-between. Share those experiences and encourage others to join you.

The sport of triathlon attracts a wide variety of people. Paris (Tennessee) recently started hosting a triathlon. In its second year it had over 250 finishers and most of those finishers were people we personally knew or recognized from other nearby races. On top of that, there were a number of people (primarily runners/cyclists) who traveled from other towns to come and cheer on the athletes. It was an amazing experience. My prediction is a number of the cheerers will be tri-ing out the triathlon next year.

Along those lines, find a guru - be a guru. It's pretty cool when you get a call from someone you helped in to the sport and they say, "Guess what? My friend wants to do a tri and they are asking me all kinds of questions. I took them on their first ride. I am now a guru!"

#108 - "Pulling a Tami" chances are scarce: so never miss one when opportunity knocks.

Midway through the triathlon bike portion, Gwin flatted. Sometimes that tire change does not go smooth. See **Law # 103**. Indeed, it took him twelve minutes to get rolling again (which according to him, of course, is the only reason I beat him that day). Apparently, a very sweet Russian girl stopped to help him. She was primarily moral support, although she did have a very nice pair of "tire levers"...never heard them called that before. Anyway, Gwin is struggling with his tire and his Russian, when Tami, his girlfriend, goes by on her bike. Instantly assessing the situation she decided there was no upside to stopping. She actually turned her head sideways and tried to shield her face in hopes Gwin would not notice her. So, there are times when "pulling a Tami" are quite acceptable - see also **Law #22.**

#109 - Muscle cramps are bonus exercise, especially while having a post work-out/race beer.

After all, a cramp is your muscles contracting to the maximum...calories are being burned. Just don't start writhing on the bar floor. Also very welcome (and less painful) are those fasciculation's/twitches. When they keep you awake at night - think of it as training and burning calories.

Be aware that if you draw attention to the muscle cramps, your triathlete friends will try to assist you - even if you don't want their help. Pickle juice with mustard, anyone? On the flipside, if your friend is experiencing muscle cramps and you laugh at their look of agony, the muscle cramp Gods will bestow a similar fate upon you. You have been warned. Also, make a note if driving after a race, cruise control is advised. A muscle cramp while going down the interstate at 75 mph can cause some serious challenges.

#110 - Weight is weight.

We agonize over each and every cycling-related purchase: how many ounces more is that component? Yet, if we lost 5% of our body weight it would be the equivalent of riding a helium bike. It is essentially common sense. The weight of the cyclist's body resists forward movement. Therefore, if the cyclist can reduce his body weight without reducing his power output, he will perform better.

Ideal weight is even more important for those hot weather races. Losing 10 pounds (of fat) is like no longer having to run in an insulated body suit.

Of course, as in any situation the general idea of this rule can be taken too far by the over compulsive athlete. To help create a balance and get a better idea of what your ideal racing weight is, read Matt Fitzgerald's book, "Racing Weight: Quick Start Guide." Fitzgerald is an acclaimed author, highly sought after coach of runners and triathletes, and sports nutritionist with a worldwide reputation. In his book he notes that maximum weight loss and maximum performance cannot be equal priorities for an endurance athlete. Even though it is true that lean athletes waste less energy, dissipate heat faster and even gain more fitness from every workout, Fitzgerald importantly notes that "too many endurance athletes try to lose weight on the same crash diets couch potatoes use, thereby sabotaging their own training and racing." Fitzgerald supplies you with a formula to calculate your ideal racing weight, but emphasizes racing weight is "defined functionally not theoretically...performance decides your true racing weight." His racing weight system is based on five principles: 1) Improve your diet quality; 2) Balance your energy sources; 3) Time nutrients; 4) Manage appetite; 5) Train for racing weight. As Fitzgerald says, "Endurance performance is a puzzle of many pieces. The attainment of optimal racing weight is one of those pieces."

But the end all point of **Law #110** is that your body weight is something you need to come to terms with to race most efficiently and effectively.

#111 - "You Are an Ironman®."

When you cross the finish line of a long course triathlon, those are some of the sweetest words you will ever hear. Right up there with, "Congratulations, it's a boy." Well, OK, or "a girl." However, half of a long course triathlon is just that. It is an accomplishment for sure, but it is not finishing a long course triathlon. It is like saying you lost your virginity, when you only got to second base. Maybe a little better than kissing your sister. See **Law #114**. Similarly, save the tattoo until after you have completed the full thing. A guy in our group got a huge IM tattoo on his shoulder long before he even entered a long course triathlon. Needless to say, he had to have a supply of even larger Band-Aids to cover it up whenever he wanted to work out with us.

#112 - Kona: it's the journey, not the destination.

The Hawaii Ironman is the holy grail of triathlon. It is also the World Championship. There are not many other sports where mere mortals have a chance to participate in the same race with the best in the world. We will never do the Olympics or The Tour. Of course, not every triathlete wants to or should aspire to do Hawaii. However, if you do and if you are not genetically blessed, it is still an attainable dream. Unfortunately, the general lottery has been deemed illegal - probably by some sorry politician who couldn't qualify. There is still the Ironman Legacy Lottery* option.

Also, there are times when Kona spots roll way on down. So, if it's your dream, pursue it and enjoy the journey. It took me 25 years and 14 "official" Ironman® distance races to finally get to Hawaii - and I wouldn't change one step of the journey.

Finally, even if you never compete in Kona, it should be on your bucket list to attend the race at least once. The feeling will last a lifetime.

*As of 2016 for the Ironman® Legacy, you must have completed a minimum of twelve full-distance IRONMAN® branded races. You must have never participated in Ironman World Championship in Kailua-Kona, Hawaii. You must have completed at least one full-distance IRONMAN® branded event the year before you enter the Ironman® Legacy and the year you enter the Ironman® Legacy. You must be registered for a full-distance Ironman® for the following year.

#113 - The finish line is just a rest stop.

It is not the final destination. It won't be long until you start planning the next phase of your journey.

So, remember be careful of what you say. If, "I'm never doing it again," crosses your lips as you cross the finish line, be prepared to eat your words. INDIA is a common reaction - but often short lived. India is one of my favorite countries to visit, probably because there are a not a great number of places to swim and thus a great excuse not to. After travelling there with Gwin, he was pretty emphatic that INDIA stands for "I'm Never Doing It Again." Very similar to thoughts you will have multiple times during (and after) a long course triathlon, for sure. But then one of our coping measures kicks in and we tend to forget the more painful parts (without this aid of nature most women would only do childbirth once). Next thing you know you are thinking about how to tweak your nutrition and training...Australia sounds inviting - "just a destination long course triathlon."

Along those lines, it is one of my pastimes while training for a long course triathlon (particularly during the last miles of a 100 miles bike ride when all my companions have dropped me) to come up with a similar acronym - I Really Ought've Not - is about as far as I get and that sums it up. Of course, as noted the next day I am right back out there.

#114 - Know your race distance.

*"A rose by any other name would smell just as sweet," is a very valid quote. However, an Ironman® called by any other name is not the same. And as mentioned in **Law #111** the title is earned and not awarded for just any race.*

So, learn the difference between race distances and call them what they are. Not all triathlons are an Ironman® – i.e. if you are doing a Sprint triathlon you cannot say you are doing an Ironman®. A Tough Mudder is not an Ironman®.

Race:	Sprint	Olympic (Intermediate)	Half Distance	Long Distance
Swim	200-750m	1500m	1.2 mi	2.4 mi
Bike	5-15 mi	24.8 mi	56 mi	112 mi
Run	1-3.1 mi	6.2 mi	13.1 mi	26.2 mi

You will undoubtedly have a friend, work colleague or family member who calls every race you do a marathon or an IM. Politely explain the difference, but do not dwell on the fact or give them flashcard reminders when they continue to call your races by the wrong terms. Be thankful for their support and don't be a "triathole" about it. They are showing an interest but will probably never do a race themselves (if they do plan on signing up for a race, please take the time to ensure they know the differences in the distances). However, as a triathlete yourself, you need to take the time to learn the race distances. Especially, if you sign up to do a race - it is helpful to know how far you need to go for each discipline so you can train accordingly.

#115 - Overtraining or lazy? Check your heart rate.

Everyone has one of "those days" during a serious training effort. Do I need to back off or push through? Know what your resting pulse is. First thing in the morning, before rolling out of bed is the best time to determine your ticker's rate. You need to do it a few mornings in a row, initially, to get your baseline. Once your baseline is established, then on a morning when you "aren't feeling it," check your resting heart rate. If it is significantly higher than your baseline, opt for an easy work out or just roll over and allow yourself to sleep in. It's cheating if you sneak in that morning coffee before checking your pulse. If you are one of those obsessive triathletes, purchase a pulse oximeter. Just hook it to your finger each morning - not only will you get your heart rate, but also your oxygen saturation (if that is low it is time to stop smoking, too).

Swim 500 - still not feeling it? Probably best to not push through. Ignore the scheduled hard work out. In the long run, it will do you more good to have an easier day. Think quality workouts not quantity. Your coach will hopefully agree.

#116 - Choose a focus...what's your mantra?

The distance of the race (or training) does not matter, at some point doubt will creep in if you let it. On a sprint it is, "I don't think that I can hold this pace another mile." During a long course, "This swim is long and I'm not sure that I can keep this up," or "I just can't run another step." While you should have mental focus points planned and practiced, this is the time to really control your mind. It is essential to practice it in training. Focusing on technique is always good. Pedal circles. Pedal a little harder with the right leg for 20 revs and then do the same for the other leg. Count your strokes on the swim. Focus on leaning forward during the run.

The running guru, Bobby McGee (involved in endurance coaching for over 32 years for both elite athletes and individual amateurs of all levels) has a great point, "Focus on what you can control." You may not be able to control how hot it is or how many miles you have left, but you can control the way your arm swings behind you or where you are looking off into the distance (not straight down) while you run. Every time your mind wanders you sacrifice form. This translates into time.

Another tip is to count - taken from, "Be Iron Fit" by Don Fink (who has coached hundreds of athletes, authored numerous training books and has completed over 30 Ironman with a PR of 9 hours 3 minutes). When you hit a rough patch, count to some predetermined number, such as 100. The act of counting will give you something to focus on besides what is bothering you and by the time you get to 100, you will have forgotten (hopefully) whatever it was. Or if you are doing a long course triathlon why not count to 140.6 and while you are at it try to recite "The Laws" associated with each mile. Just don't get too distracted so that you forget **Law #0.6**.

"Triathlete EQ: A Guide for Emotional Endurance" by Dr. Izzy Justice is a good source for practicing mental toughness and focus for triathletes.

Choose a focus and next thing you know, "this too has passed."

#117 - Flow: It may be elusive, but the quest is well worth it.

Read *"The Rise of Superman: Decoding the Science of Ultimate Human Performance,"* by Steven Kotler. It is amazing what humans can achieve when in the state of "flow" and this certainly holds true for training and racing triathlons.

"Flow" is biking a century and it's over before you know it. "Flow" is driving through Manhattan during rush hour and every traffic light is green while you weave through traffic, not once touching your brakes. Mihaly Csikszentmihalyi a Hungarian psychologist popularized the psychological concept of "flow." He first described it in *Flow: The Psychology of Optimal Experience."* I really can't explain "flow" anywhere near as well as Mihaly does, but then I can't even pronounce his name. Paradoxically, you will not be aware that you are in a state of "flow" during a race or workout. However, you will know afterwards and it is pretty cool.

#118 - Medical advice: take it or leave it.

No disrespect intended towards the medical profession, after all I am a member. However, most medical providers do not have a great grasp on what is involved with triathlons. Years ago, my "man's best friend" decided to chase a cat during one of our morning runs. Unfortunately, my knee was in the direct path of his route and my medial meniscus lost the confrontation. Impatient with my recovery and unhappy with the brace I was supposed to wear, I consulted several respected orthopedists. The approach was sadly very similar. A look at my knees, followed by a look at the x-rays and MRI, a shake of the head culminated in a, "No more running for you." When I mentioned the long course triathlon and the marathon that I was already signed up for (i.e. committed to) there was more dubious shaking of the head. The advice centered more on when a good time for the knee replacement might be. Not really what I wanted to hear.

Since then I have completed eight more long course races, multiple other triathlons and marathons. Wearing the knee brace was awkward at best. Its main function was to keep some of the pressure off my medial, inner left knee. I realized I could achieve the same effect by running on the right side of the road - no problem as long as I picked a road with little traffic. So, good bye knee brace. Throw in some pool running, some slower miles, more gradual mileage increases, more willingness to shorten some planned workouts, losing some pounds - and the body does an amazing job of mending and adapting.

The bottom line is that it's your body. No one knows it better. You are a pretty good judge of what is possible.

"Running Strong" by Dr. Jordan Metzl (nationally recognized sports medicine physician, best-selling author and fitness instructor) has an interesting take on this. While Dr. Metzl was in med school, he tore his ACL while playing soccer. He had always been an avid athlete and based on his diagnosis, surgery and recovery it encouraged him to focus on sports medicine. In particular he seeks to help runners recover from and prevent injuries. The goal is to enjoy running well into the 80's. It is an interesting read and includes an excellent strength training workout based on functional fitness moves that mimic running motions and strengthen areas that tend to be weak - glutes, hips, etc - to help strengthen your kinetic chain. He also notes that, "If something is bothering you and makes you change the way you are running, stop."

Do preventative maintenance and prevent those injuries. *Another book very worth reading is Dr. Kelly Starrett's "Ready to Run." Dr. Starrett is a physical therapist and owner of San Francisco Crossfit, the first such gym to incorporate an on-site physical therapy practice. In "Ready to Run," he details certain standards we should be able to reach/maintain in order to prevent running injuries. He then details exercises to reach these standards. He also stresses the importance of listening to your body - so that if you feel a "twinge" in your Achilles - don't just push through and ignore it. Dr. Starrett addresses how to treat a small twinge and prevent it from becoming a major tear or injury.*

Personally, 2014 was a year of a frustrating Achilles tendinitis - slowing down, cutting back, getting a little better, chiropractic adjustments, medical visits, reinjuring and repeat. My daughters insisted I read *Ready to Run.* Following some of the exercises and Starrett's advice has resolved that nagging injury.

We have all been there and pushed through to suffer an injury. So, listen to your body and prevent those injuries before they become serious.

By the way - Having a joint replacement does not mean the end of your triathlon career. David Miller not only completed but won his 65-69 year age group at the Escape from Alcatraz in 2015, with two artificial hips.

#119 - Triathlon is a lifelong activity.

Sure not everyone is Lew Hollander finishing his 58th long course triathlon at age 84. As a side note, Hollander only started competing in triathlons at the age of 55.

Along those lines, Sister Madonna Buder holds the world record for the oldest woman (as of 2015) to ever finish a long course triathlon (Ironman Canada at the age of 82). The "Iron Nun" is still competing in triathlons and has done more than 340 triathlons, with over 45 of them long course triathlons. She started running at the age of 47 and did her first long course at the age of 75. What was your excuse?

So age, per se, is not a limitation. In fact, according to USAT, 900 of its annual memberships are over 80 years old and 5% of its total membership are 60 plus.

In terms of "staying young" regardless of your age, an excellent read is *"Younger Next Year"* by Chris Chowley and Henry S. Lodge M.D. Swimming, biking and/or running is a great start to help keep aging at bay. Add in some weight lifting for 30 minutes three times a week, watch your diet, don't drink alcohol in excess (well, at least not in frequent excess) and have some good friends. Stay active and you will stay younger.

#120 - You can be old and still be fast.

Yes, we slow down as we age. However, we do not need to slow down nearly as much as expected. The key to not losing speed is to include weekly high intensity workouts. *"Fast after Fifty"* by Joe Friel (endurance athlete coach, author of numerous books and founder of the USA Triathlon National Coaching Commission) explains it well. Friel notes that while aerobic capacity (VO2 max) does decline with age, one of the main reasons we slow down is that most athletes over the age of 50 gravitate towards long, slow distance (LSD) training. "In those aging athletes who continue to do High-Intensity Interval Training aerobic capacity drops slowly, at a rate of about half a percent per year, until the mid-seventies when it accelerates. Athletes training primarily with LSD see a decline of about 1 to

1.5 percent per year." Friel goes into much more detail and helps you develop your training utilizing this approach. On the other hand children of the 60's had some good times with LSD (so I've heard).

"Born to Run" by Christopher McDougall reinforces the point that you can be older and still be fast. In this book that provides sensational running inspiration with the support of cutting edge science, Professor Dennis Bramble presents research in which they analyzed the results from the 2004 NYC Marathon, comparing finishing times by age. Starting at the age of 19 you get faster every year, until you hit your peak at age 27. After 27, your speed starts to decline. Dr. Bramble asks the question, "How old are you when you're back to running at the same speed you did at 19?" The answer: Sixty-four years old.

#121 - No one can ever take it away from you.

After you finish your first long course triathlon - you will always be an Ironman®. It will be one of the hardest things you will ever do in your life. The experience will help see you through the next time you have to do extra overtime at work or complete a task that seems insurmountable. The IM accomplishment will be in the back of your mind - consciously or subconsciously, you know these four hours of OT are a piece of cake.

Break it down the same way you would a long course triathlon, one little piece at a time instead of thinking about the whole project. Little by little you will get there and you won't even have to pee your pants to arrive (hopefully not, but if you do, good thing you are an experienced Ironman®).

#122 - Cheer in the last finisher - at least once.

Listening to Mike Reilly work the crowd as the clock winds down to midnight is a priceless memory. The last finisher has been out there for over 16 hours and they are giving it their all for those last yards that stretch on forever. In Hawaii many of the pros are at the finish line - celebrating their own season as well as the last finishers. 140.6 is a distance that unites everyone.

#123 - Recovery days needed after a race equal the number of miles of the run.

This is a general rule of runners and it seems to hold true for triathlon as well. One would think that recovery after a long course triathlon would be longer than "just" a marathon. However, universally one is sorer after a hard marathon. It has to do with the intensity of the 26.2. That is not to say that you can race long course every month and do well. Recovery is also dependent on where you are in your training life. Expect that recovery after your first long course triathlon will be longer then if you have completed several during the recent years. If in doubt take another easy day.

Take advantage of that recovery and milk it for all it's worth, you earned it!

The pros even stress the importance of recovery. Mark Allen, Ironman World Champion (1989-93, 1995) notes that it is important to take some time off at the end of your season, particularly if you put a lot of energy into your training and racing. "The biggest mistake people make is they do their last race of the year, take two weeks easy and then they're back training at full speed. In two weeks you're not able to put back all the energy that you took out during 10 months of training hard." You should still keep active, but don't do structured training.

Mental recovery may well take longer than physical recovery. It's hard to have much of a life/relationship when seriously training for a long course triathlon - especially if also holding down a job. Your body may be feeling pretty good after three weeks - your marriage may need a little more time. Give it time.

#124 - Less is more...well for some aspects of triathlon.

Many triathletes are a little compulsive *(understatement of the year)*. They plan every minute of their day - right up to the starting line. On the days before a long course race, during that taper, there is very little you can do to make yourself faster. There is a lot you can do to make your race day longer/slower or even injure yourself. So, do less. If your schedule calls for a 20 minute swim the day before the race, and you don't feel like it...then don't swim. Rest. Sit instead of standing. Lie down instead of sitting. Walk instead of run. Rest in the days before is the most important thing you can do to give yourself the best race day. Friends and family will want to cheer you on. Let them know that you are not going to be sight-seeing or going out for late big dinners. Rest.

#125 - There is no such thing as bad weather for training: just bad choice of clothing.

There is no guarantee that race day weather will be perfect. Probably a "Law" that it will not be. So, train in bad weather. No excuses. *If you only train on nice, sunny days you can bet your bottom dollar that your race day is going to be cold, windy and drizzly* (at the best). You need to train in all kinds of weather so you are ready and capable to handle all that comes your way race day. You can believe your competitors don't let a little shower or a cool morning knock them off their training plan.

#126 - Be inspired.

Many times you will meet a "handicapped" triathlete - often as they are passing you. Think of the obstacles they have overcome just to reach the starting line. Cheer them on - even if you are silently hoping for a steep up hill to pull that wheelchair girl back into sight. For the ones that have them - cheer their guides/handlers on as well. At mile 16 of Ironman New York City a visually impaired runner and his guide passed me going up a hill. I said something about being strong and picking up the pace for the last miles. The runner thanked me. The struggling guide gave me a look and put his finger to his lips gesturing me to hush.

#127 - Have fun while training.

It's OK to stop and have a corn dog in the middle of that century ride. In these days of coaches, power meters, heart rate zones and set workouts, take some time to have an easy ride or run with friends.

Even the pro triathletes will tell you that it is good to do some training without your watch at all. Yes, shock-horror! Ironman World Champion Leanda Cave (2012) advises, "Go out for a run or ride and leave the watch or bike computer at home. Take some money with you and find a destination on a map and make that your goal. Treat yourself with a coffee and/or bite to eat and sit around for a bit and think to yourself how amazing it is that you have the ability to do such a wonderful thing. Being grateful every now and then can keep you more motivated than anything anyone can say or do."

Not only will it allow you to spend more quality time with yourself or your training partners, but it can also help you learn how to listen to your body. There will be a time when your watch does not work. This does not mean time has stopped. Don't let it mess up your race.

#128 - Be kind to newbies.

It's fun to introduce others to the "ins" and "outs" of the sport. Just remember that many of them may be faster than you one day - sometimes much sooner than you would like. So, encourage them and if you have to drop them on a hill every once in a while, let them catch up again. Be a good tri-ambassador.

On the flip side, once you become faster than the person who introduced you to triathlon, remember your beginnings. Remember how that person waited for you to catch up and didn't razz you too much about it. You should do the same (a plea from the old guy).

#129 - Keep the details to yourself.

Others do not want to hear the intricate details about your latest training ride or race. Their eyes glaze over when you start talking about swimming a mile. As Facebook posts go - let me know when you wreck (and if your bike is okay, see **Law #37**), but otherwise spare me the workout details and the pictures of your Garmin.

We eat, breathe and dream this stuff, but we are in the minority (albeit the fitter minority). So, just as you don't enjoy reading posts about your Facebook friend's morning sickness, no one really wants to hear about what heart rate/pace you held "x" number of miles. If you are in company of other triathletes it might be acceptable to share these details, particularly if you all did the same training ride or race. For the rest of the population going into too much detail makes you look like a "triathole." On a side note, if you were a lot faster than you training companions or fellow racers, they may not want to hear the details of just how fast you were either. Common courtesy goes a long way.

#130 - Tri a new tri.

One of the greatest things about triathlon is that amateurs can do almost all the pro races. We can do the World Series or participate in the equivalent of the "Super Bowl" for triathletes. So, give some of these races a tri. We have included a list of some of our favorites in the Appendix.

The popular ones fill early/are difficult to get into, but it is not always as hard as it is reputed to be to get a slot. In 2015, we had a group of six that tried for a lottery slot for the Escape from Alcatraz. Five of us got a slot and the sixth got in via a fund raiser.

You will never know if you don't tri.

#131 - Coaches are optional.

A good coach - one who is competent and on the same page with you - is a great coach to have. Good coaches stay current and understand effective training and racing. If you are a beginner it helps with learning the ropes. If you are a veteran who has plateaued or is slipping downhill a little - a coach might be good for you. Frequently injuring yourself - might be a good idea to get help. Nothing wrong with just doing your own thing though. It is kind of fun to tune into your own body and discover your own limits. Still, the more serious you are about achieving your potential in racing, the more important a coach will be.

#132 - There is equality between female and male.

It was not until the 75th running of the Boston Marathon that the first official female entrant was allowed. You don't see much of the women's Tour de France but it does exist. The first International Triathlon Union race was held in Avignon France 1989. After the athletes arrived the organizers announced that the male prize money would be more than the females'. The males protested and refused to race until the organizers relented. Ever since this first world championship the prize money has always been equal.

#133 - Be at peace.

The aforementioned running guru, Bobby McGee passed along another piece of advice at one of his training camps: An argument with the spouse the night before a race is the equivalent of riding a hard time trial.

It's a good time to capitulate early and prevent a blowout...it was probably your fault anyway.

#134 - Check out the course.

The unknown increases anxiety. Next time you are at the start of a race you did the previous year - compare the feeling to being at the start of a race you are doing for the first time. There is a significantly different level of stress. So take the time to read the course descriptions - surprise there are 5 flights of stairs! *Social media is a good source for obtaining information. If you are able - get there early and drive the parts of the course that you can. Better still, if the site is close enough, do some of your training rides/runs/swims on the course. If the swim is not accessible to the public, consider attending one of the sponsored swim sessions. Knowledge is power and reduces stress.*

#135 - Vaseline® is your friend.

Use it liberally on all those areas that rub you the wrong way. Just don't eat it! *I have a friend who was doing his first marathon and everyone before the race kept telling him to make sure he had enough salt during the race; otherwise he would become the victim of cramps. This is the key piece of advice that stuck in his head. While he was running along, feeling great, he remembered the salt advice and thought he should probably grab some. Most aid stations along the course had salt pills, along with the usual Gatorade, water, gels and Vaseline® on a stick. I guess the salt must have been next to the Vaseline®. He heard "Salt" and grabbed the Vaseline® on the stick. He proceeded to place the whole glop in his mouth. It was a wonder he was able to swallow it without vomiting. I guess it helped lubricate his lungs as he finished smooth with no cramps.*

#136 - The pain doesn't get less as you train more - you just get faster or go longer.

Or as you get older - you don't slow down quite as much.

#137 - Triathlon is not life or death.

Sure it feels that way at times. Rarely do we lose a friend in training or a race, but at no higher frequency then the normal toll of accidents and nature's laws. So maintain a sense of perspective in your triathlon world. Keeping a balance in your triathlon, personal and work life will result in support rather than resentment and problems. In the long run (or swim) it will increase your enjoyment of the sport.

#138 - Don't pick favorites.

Focus on what you are bad at. Love to bike? Swimming is okay? Hate the run? You should be spending more time on perfecting your run and swim than the bike. Though, you should not completely ignore the bike. It is a balancing act. We have three sports we are competing in. If you want to be good at triathlon you need to be good in all three events. Being excellent in one, will not make you the winner.

Race your strengths, train your weaknesses.

#139 - It's OK to wear a Speedo - if it's OK.

Just like some women shouldn't wear bikinis or go topless, some guys should stick with trisuits (not too tight or too worn). Back in the 1980's, Mrs. T's Triathlon in downtown Chicago was the world's largest. The finish was about a mile from transition. After the race my good friend Ron and I were walking back to the transition on a fine Sunday, late morning, a beer in each hand. Ron with his swimming background sported a suit not much larger than a g-string. I was decked out in my "full size" tie-dyed Speedo. No shirts. The cop graciously waved us across the intersection - six lanes of stopped traffic with little old ladies on their way home from church. We were oblivious until the honking started. At least one of us looked good in their Speedo ;)

#140 - Get out the door.

On a recent Saturday morning my schedule only called for an easy one hour run, but I wasn't feeling it. Instead I was eating junk food and about to crack a cold one. The run was not going to happen. Then I got a text from Ron. Swimming is his passion and years ago he was my swimming guru. While we stay in touch he has moved to Ohio and we rarely see each other. Two years ago he noticed his swim times slowing. Eventually he was diagnosed with ALS. Now he was texting me about how he finally had to give up his job and that the wheelchair was in place. Then he said he was on the way to the pool. "I can still kick pretty well. I have to use the slow lane, but give the old guys a run for the money. They love to try and beat me." I put my beer back in the fridge and was out the door.

#140.6

The common denominator of all triathletes is **Law #0.6**. Angela Duckworth calls it being "gritty" in her bestseller "*Grit the Power of Passion and Perseverance.*" Our clocks keep ticking - the choice is ours. Move or not. Choose onwards and get the most out of your journey.

"It ain't about how hard you hit, it's about how hard you can get hit. And keep moving forward. It's how much you can take. And keep moving forward. That's how winning is done."
- Rocky

And winning doesn't mean getting to the finish line first. Walter Payton has a great definition of what it means to be a winner...

"...You know what a winner is? A winner is somebody who has given his best effort, who has tried the hardest they possibly can, who has utilized every ounce of energy and strength within them to accomplish something. It doesn't mean that they accomplished it or failed, it means that they've given it their best. That's a winner."
- Walter Payton,
"Never Die Easy: The Autobiography of Walter Payton"

So, remember **#0.6** and you will be a winner.

Appendix

Personal "Bucket List" Favorites

Too many races and too few weekends. Here is my personal baker's dozen based on anything from having a down river swim to having won the age group there once upon a time. Some are included as they are so memorable, others because they are our tradition - and yes, we often wonder why. While some on this list sell out - they are certainly in reach for anyone motivated to participate.

IM Florida, Panama City Beach, Florida has a great setting for the family and the bonus of getting some beach time *and pina colodas*. It features a swim that does justice to the sport. Organizers are more safety conscious these days and on occasion have cancelled the swim. Otherwise for a sporty swim: waves, current, salt water, wet suits, mass start - it is the best. The bike is fast, hot, flat and windy - which is OK. The run loops through the park twice and it is always fun to point out a gator to your neighbor and watch the pace pick up. You can capture the same race feeling with the Gulf Coast (aka Gulf Roast) half IM in May (same location), though it sadly no longer loops through the park.

The White Sands Sprint, Panama City Beach, Florida takes place in November making it the ideal season finale. It is short. It is fun. The swim-to-bike run to the transition goes through the middle of Spinnaker's Bar and the drinks (post-race) are free. *This is actually part of a series. They do the same race at the beginning of the season, so you can do both and compare your times. We found and participated in the second one because I was determined we needed an "end of the season" race and there were certain requirements: good location (the beach), only a sprint option (so no one felt they had to go longer), a Saturday race so we could spend Saturday afternoon on the beach (and not worry about dehydrating before the race) and good after party (awesome door prizes and free drinks at Spinnakers when the race finishes by 9:00 a.m. what more could you want). Another interesting aspect of the race is that if you are female you can* *pay an extra $5 and start in the first wave. The top three females that finish ahead of any males are awarded prize money.*

The New York City Olympic Triathlon, New York City, New York. The run is always memorable through upper Manhattan and Central Park. However, the real thrill is the swim. Salt water, with the tide, wet suit...my swim time was 15 minutes (half my usual 30). The tough thing was finding something to do with the rest of our time in the city ;). *The most memorable aspect of the race for me is the spectators and cheerers. It is amazing how they can make such a difference in your overall race experience. I also remember an awesome post-race mimosa and meal.*

The Paris Triathlon. That would be Paris, Tennessee. Not only is it our closest, but it is a sprint without an Olympic option. The water is about as clean as it gets in Tennessee. *So, bring your q-tips for afterwards.* The bike includes a mile long bridge over the Tennessee River and some rolling hills through the park. The run circles the local harbor area. Post-race it is off to the pavilion for all you can eat catfish and hush puppies. Trophies feature a catfish. Yes, Paris is the "world's catfish capital" - take that, France!

Music City, Nashville, Tennessee is the country's second oldest continuously run triathlon. It is a well-organized event set up by Team Magic (who organizes numerous races including the Chattanooga Tri). The transition area is usually adjacent to the Titan's football stadium. It is probably the only time that anyone swims in the Cumberland River downtown Nashville, for good reason. There is always the suspense of the "unknown" regarding the river. One year a flood of water was released prior to race start and the water temp dropped from 82 the night before to 72 race morning. See **Law #8.** So many of the sprint participants got swept away that their swim was cancelled mid event. *Quite the spectacle watching and a little unnerving for the first time participants doing the Olympic distance, which starts after the Sprint.* The bike is on a four lane highway closed to traffic (and shade). The run sometimes *(there have been some changes to the course throughout the years)* goes through downtown, winding past the bars as patrons are heading in - good fun *and great smells.* Other times, the run has looped through an industrial wasteland (only shade from one tree and an overpass) as the asphalt melts. Great view of the city skyline and the "Batman building" on the return loop though. Hey - it's a tradition.

IM Coeur d'Alene, Coeur d'Alene, Idaho. At least once experience having to swim while wearing booties and an insulated swim cap. Don't worry - the shivering stops by mile 20 of the bike as you race up your first mountain. Scenic and laid back.

The Mach Tenn, Tulahoma, Tennessee is another small field, local, sprint only tri. Well organized with parts of the course venturing into the local military base. It features fresh grilled burgers and limitless free beer. Need I say more?

Memphis in May (MIM), Millington, Tennessee is our other traditional tri. Currently, the race is a mere shadow of its glory days. Having to change race locations and venue uncertainties will do that to a race. Still we are cheering for a comeback. MIM continues to provide excellent organization, live music, southern food, limitless free beer and of course Elvis (who ceremoniously accompanies the last finisher on their run across the levy to the line).

IM Mont-Tremblant, Mont-Tremblant, Quebec, Canada. You have not lived until you ingest a Beaver Tail fresh from the fryer in Tremblant. The swim, the bike, the run are all picturesque. Of course, they also serve beaver tails year round so the half distance triathlon is an equally good choice.

Gravenhurst Triathlon, Gravenhurst, Ontario, Canada. Pick the sprint or the Olympic or both. The start is inspired by Alcatraz. Two of the last functioning steamers take you 1500 meters out to the start and you swim back to shore.

Open water swims in Ontario are always astounding to triathletes who have only raced in the south. Yes, you can see your outstretched hand. Yes, that is the lake bottom you see. Yes, it is twelve feet down. The bike is scenic and goes by the Muskoka Brewing Company - well worth stopping in for free tastings (better after the race). They limit the race to 300 people so catch the start of registration.

Escape from Alcatraz Triathlon, San Francisco, California. Epic. This race has it all for a triathlon. Great location, history, fear, suspense, and excitement. Did those guys really escape? Will I get swept out to sea as they did? Did someone say shark? Golden Gate Bridge in the fog. Sand Ladder. A full day of memories. And, yet, it is very doable for most triathletes. Get yourself signed up and just do it.

Alpe d'Huez Triathlon, Alpe d'Huez, France. Do the Olympic distance - why spoil it with multiple mountains on the long course? Stay near the finish line and bike to the start. It is the only race where I biked over ten miles to the start and never pedaled once. Count the hair pin turns while "racing" up the mountain. Think of the epic stages of the Tour. Then do your 10 K at altitude. *Still on my "bucket list" as I was only a spectator at this event. However, the escargot and the kir royale we dined on while watching the event were superb.*

IM Lanzarote, Canarias, Spain. Crystal clear water, biking through lava fields, winding up and up into the clouds to the tip of the volcano and back down to the ocean. Of all the races I've completed this is the most scenic. If it wasn't so darn hard, long, far and expensive I would love to do it annually.

My add-on (I mean if we are going to have a baker's dozen might as well throw in a few donut holes):

IM Arizona, Tempe, Arizona. *Held in November the weather is usually very nice (especially compared to any races done in the southern United States). The mass start swim is NOT fun, but when are they ever? At least it is in a* closed body of water with little current and no fear of sharks. The bike is a couple loops of a flat and fast course with only one hill that helps break up the ride. The back drop of cacti and dessert landscape make for some good "official" race photos. The run is two loops, flat and FULL of spectators that cheer you on with such enthusiasm you can't help but smile. Until this day it remains my fastest long course triathlon and the one that I had the most "fun" at.

USAT Nationals (location varies year-to-year). *I have been lucky enough to participate at this event for a number of years at various locations. Despite where it may be, one thing remains the same - the event is well organized and caters to the athletes as if they were royalty. It is pretty cool to earn a spot at USAT Olympic nationals (you must be in the top 10% of your age group at a qualifying triathlon - most USAT events are qualifying events). Even if you feel like you are "not worthy" you would be amazed at the variety of participants. One of the reasons why triathlon is so great - you are worthy whatever your ability. If you can't qualify for the Olympic you can still participate in the Sprint (it is an open event), but let me warn you don't expect the competition to be any less. Most athletes do both the Olympic and the Sprint. But as previously noted not everyone is "Hardcore."*

The "General" Check List

Clothing (essential):

Guys - Racechip. If it is your first tri and you think it may be your last one, then wear your swim suit or bike shorts and put on a T-shirt after the swim *(most races do not let you go shirtless)*. Try not to wear real baggy shorts on the bike - baggy shorts are not aero and scream out "this is my first tri." Otherwise a tri suit is what you need. *Please ensure to check that your tri suit is not well worn. Yes, you need to have worn it for a number of your training rides but see through does not mean more aero.* Consider layering with some old throw away clothes for pre-race. Have some clean clothes for after. Towel and soap/shampoo are an option.

Gals - Racechip. *Experiment with different clothing options and find what works best for you. As with all women's clothing, different companies have different standards when it comes to size. Just because you typically wear a medium shirt does not mean you will always wear a medium tri shirt. Trisuits are available for women (and usually run small!) and many women love them. I personally have to use the bathroom too many times before race start and I don't like unzipping myself and nearly getting in the nude to do so, especially in a porta potty. But like I said personal preference is key and trisuits are more "aero." Same goes for "to wear" or "not to wear" the sports bra as some jerseys have built in bra options. Definitely a personal preference and one you should have practiced if you plan to go without come race day. Same as guys when it comes to layering on some throw away clothes for prerace. Sometimes there is a walk to the swim start so old shoes or at least an old pair of socks are nice to have. Typically there is a place to shower after the smaller races and it is nice to clean up afterwards, so bring clean clothes, towel, soap/shampoo/conditioner, etc.*

Gear bag - a backpack works just fine and often you can ride your bike to transition (just remember to wear your helmet). Some people use 5 gallon buckets to carry their gear, but...

Since the Boston Marathon bombings, some of the bigger races have gotten a lot stricter in what you can bring/leave in transition. Oftentimes, they won't let you bring a big back pack. Instead they give you a clear plastic bag for all your transition needs. If you are biking to the start you can typically put the plastic bag in a small drawstring back pack to help you carry your stuff. Then, when you get to transition, put the drawstring bag in the clear plastic bag. Beware, if you do bring a back pack in (when they let you), you may not be allowed to leave it in transition, so you will have to check it at the gear check station. Know where the gear check station is and leave yourself some time to sort that out, as often it is not right at the start and there may be a line.

Swim - goggles, nose or ear plugs (if you use them), swim cap, wet suit, *anti-chafe ointment.*

Bike - helmet, sunglasses, bike shoes, tire pump, and your bike. Generally no bike gloves unless you are a cyclist.

Run - running shoes, socks, hat.

Nutrition - Water bottles for bike. If you are doing a race shorter than an Olympic, you really should not need 10 gels taped to your bike, a couple should be plenty. However, by race day you should have an idea based on your training. Hand held water bottle if you use it. Prerace snack and sports drink bottle to carry with you out of transition. *I usually have just a plain, store bought plastic bottle of water in transition in a small, iced down cooler for the hotter races. That way I can grab water once I am heading out on the run and drink/pour it on my head as needed. Usually there is an aid station with water on your way out of transition. However, I have been to a race before where it was miles down the road - it was hot and I was thirsty.*

Transition - race belt, number, safety pins, towel *(make sure you check with race as some races no longer let you have a towel)* to set your gear on (and save your spot on the rack if you remove your bike pre-race), sun screen, sharpie.

Long Course Triathlon Check List

Hopefully you have developed your own list. You will need to use the race given gear bags and special needs bags. Nothing can be left in transition but your bike - which has to be in transition the day before the race. Your gear bags need to be dropped off the day before the race as well. You usually do have access to your bike and bags on race morning to add water bottles, nutrition and pump tires. Special needs bags are dropped off the morning of the race. Nutrition/fluids are usually available on the course every 10 miles for the bike and every mile for the run. Check out your athlete information provided by the specific race. Try out their gels/liquids in training to be sure they agree with you.

Your bike, run and morning clothes bags are available for pick up after the race along with your bike. Things put in your special needs bags are not returned. When you are in the change tent and have emptied out your bike bag - you put your swim stuff in it and give it to a volunteer. Similarly your run bag is used for that nasty bike stuff.

Bike bag - put your bike gear in here - except the pump - hand the pump to a friend as you leave transition pre-race. If you plan to change out of a swim suit add the clothes you plan to wear on the bike. Vaseline® and sun screen are provided by volunteers in the change tent area.

Run bag - put your run gear in here along with any nutritional needs such as a hand held water bottle.

Special needs bike - for your nutrition. Think variety and small amounts - see **Nutrition Laws**. Consider ice packs if you are including water bottles. *Some people put an extra tube and/or CO2 cartridge just in case they have used up the spare they have stashed on their bikes. Remember that these bags are typically handed off to you while you are riding by the volunteers - good idea to practice at other events.*

Special needs run - for your nutrition. Also extra clothing if there is any chance it will get chilly while you are out there in the dark finishing your race. Consider a head lamp.

Morning clothes bag - whatever clothes you want back after the race. Often nice to have at the finish.

Recommended Books

"The Rules: The Way of the Cycling Disciple" by the Velominati Keepers of the Cog

"Ready to Run" by Dr. Kelly Starrett

"Roll Model" by Jill Miller

"Never a Bad Day" by Bob Babbitt

"Born to Run" by Christopher McDougall

"A Life Without Limits" by Chrissie Wellington

"Triathlete EQ: A Guide for Emotional Endurance" by Dr. Izzy Justice

"Racing Weight: Quick Start Guide" by Matt Fitzgerald

"Be Iron Fit" by Don Fink

"The Rise of Superman: Decoding the Science of Ultimate Human Performance" by Steven Kotler

"Flow: The Psychology of Optimal Experience" by Mihaly Csikszentmihalyi

"Faster after Fifty" by Joe Friel

"Running Strong" by Dr. Jordan Metzl

"Younger Next Year" by Chris Chowley and Dr. Henry S. Lodge

"Grit: the Power of Passion and Perseverance" by Angela Duckworth